Contents

Age-Appropriate Skills

Language

- following directions
- story comprehension
- descriptive and comparative language
- rhyming
- categorization
- letter and sound recognition
- statements and questions
- auditory and visual memory
- left to right tracking
- oral language
- vocabulary and concept development
- sequencing
- color words

Math

- counting to 20
- patterning
- numeral recognition
- geometric shapes
- ordinal numbers
- beginning computation
- one-to-one matching
- graphing
- measurement

Circle-Time Books

Making Circle-Time Books ....

Follow these simple directions to assemble a circle-time book for each of the five sections of *The Farm*.

- Tear out and laminate the color story pages for each circle-time book.

- Bind the books with binder rings or an alternative binding method.

- Read the circle-time book as the opening activity for each section of *The Farm*.

Place the book on an easel or chalkboard stand and flip the pages for easy reading.

Sharing Circle-Time Books ....

Each circle-time story introduces the topic of that section. Begin by reading the story to the children several times. The first time you read it, you might ask children to predict what the story will be about by looking at the cover illustration. In subsequent readings, use strategies such as:

- moving your finger under words as you read to model left to right tracking

- allowing children to "read" the predictable text

- asking children to identify objects in the pictures

- talking about any rhyming words

- asking children to predict what will happen next in the story

- asking questions to help children recall story details

- asking at least one question that relates to children's own lives

Circle-Time Books

"Welcome to the Farm!" (pages 13–22)
Use this colorful book to introduce children to the farm unit. Pause on each page and discuss the illustrations. Allow children to share what they know about farms. Explain to children that they will be learning all about the animals on the farm, the people who live and work on the farm, and the crops that grow on the farm.

Ask questions such as:

- Why do you think the farmer said, "Put on your hat"?
- Which jobs do you think the workers might do on the farm?
- How can machines help the farmer?
- What kinds of crops grow on this farm?
- If you lived on a farm, which job would you want to do?

Section Two
People on the Farm

"A Busy Day on the Farm" (pages 53–62)
This story introduces children to a typical workday on a family farm. It is written in sequential order, proceeding from morning to night. Discuss the story with children. Contrast a day on the farm to a typical day in your own classroom or students' homes.

Ask questions such as:

- Which work did Farmer Brown do? (the children? Mrs. Brown?)
- What did Farmer Brown's family do for fun after the day's work was done?
- Who had a busy day on the farm?
- How is Farmer Brown's day different from yours?

Section Three
Animals on the Farm

"Old MacDonald Had a Farm" (pages 89–98)
This classic children's song introduces some of the animals on the farm and the sounds they make. As you read or sing the text, ask children to point to each of the animals and make the same sound the animal would make. Read the story several times. Alternate between reading the story and singing the story.

Ask questions such as:

- Can you name all the animals on Old MacDonald's farm?
- Who can name one of the animals and make its sound?
- Which of Old MacDonald's animals have you actually seen and heard?
- What other animals might be on a farm? What sound does that animal make?

Circle-Time Books

Section Four
Things That Grow on the Farm

"Harvest Time!" (pages 129–138)
This repetitive story introduces children to some of the fruits and vegetables commonly grown on farms. As you read about the different crops, talk about where each crop grows (orchard, field, garden, tree, vines, etc). Ask children to point to the fruits and vegetables pictured. Discuss which fruits and vegetables children have tasted and which are their favorites. Bring in examples of the fruits and vegetables from the story. Have a "tasting time" when children taste the different fruits and vegetables.

Ask questions such as:

- What happens at harvest time?
- Who knows the word that means that a fruit or vegetable is ready to pick?
- Are there any foods in the story that you have never eaten?
- Which is your favorite fruit/vegetable?

Section Five
From My Farm to Your House

"The Apple's Adventure" (pages 163–172)
This story uses a simple rhyme to explain an apple's journey from the time it is a tiny seed until it is picked, shipped, and finally eaten. A trip to a local supermarket to view the produce section is a great follow-up to this story.

Ask questions such as:

- What happened to the seed after it was planted?
- What happened to the apples after they were ripe?
- What happened to the apple after it was bought?
- Can you name other fruits that grow on trees like apples do?

Take-Home Books

Use these simple directions to make reproducible take-home books for each of the five sections of *The Farm*.

1. Reproduce the book pages for each child.
2. Cut the pages along the cut lines.
3. Place the pages in order, or this may be done as a sequencing activity with children. Guide children in assembling the book page by page.
4. Staple the book together.

After making each take-home book, review the story as children turn the pages of their own books. Send the storybook home along with the Parent Letter on page 5.

Dear Parent(s) or Guardian(s),

As part of our unit *The Farm*, I will be presenting five storybooks to the class. Your child will receive a take-home storybook for you to share. Remember that reading to children helps them develop a love of reading. Regularly reading aloud to children has proven to enhance a variety of early language skills, including:

- vocabulary and concept development,
- letter recognition,
- phonemic awareness,
- auditory and visual discrimination, and
- left to right tracking.

I hope you enjoy sharing these stories with your child.

As you read to your child, remember to:

1. speak clearly and with interest.
2. track words by moving your finger under each word as you read it.
3. ask your child to help you identify objects in the pictures. Talk about these objects together.
4. discuss your own experiences as they relate to the story.
5. allow your child to express his or her own thoughts and ideas and to ask you questions.

I hope you enjoy all five of these stories.

Sincerely,

_____

Storyboards

A storyboard is an excellent way to enhance vocabulary and concept development.

Each section of *The Farm* includes full-color storyboard pieces to use in extending the language and concepts introduced. Ideas for using the storyboard pieces in each section are found on pages 7–9.

Turn the full-color cutouts into pieces that will adhere to a flannel- or felt-covered storyboard. Just laminate the pieces and affix self-sticking Velcro® dots to the back of each piece.

Welcome to the Farm!
pages 29–33

People on the Farm
pages 69–73

Animals on the Farm
pages 105–109

Things That Grow on the Farm
pages 145 and 147

From My Farm to Your House
pages 179 and 181

Storyboards

"Welcome to the Farm!" Storyboard Use the colorful storyboard pieces on pages 29–33 to follow up your presentation of the story "Welcome to the Farm!" You may choose to use the following teacher script to present the story:

> *Today we are going to put together a farm storyboard. I am going to show you different places and things found on a farm. We will talk about them.*
>
>
> • *Here are some people you might recognize.*
> • *Here is the farmer. He works on the farm.*
> • *Here is the barn where the farmer keeps the hay and where some of the animals sleep.*
> • *Here are two of the crops that the farmer grows—apples and turnips.*
> • *Here are the chickens. They like to eat seeds.*
> • *Here is the pigpen where the pigs live.*
> • *Here is the meadow where the cows and the sheep graze.*
> • *Here is the farmer's family. They live on the farm.*
> • *Here are the farm workers. They perform many jobs on the farm.*

Remove the storyboard pieces and allow children to replace each piece as they retell the story.

"A Busy Day on the Farm" Storyboard Use the colorful storyboard pieces on pages 69–73 to follow up your presentation of the story "A Busy Day on the Farm." You may choose to use the following teacher script to present the story:

> • *Here is the rooster. The rooster crows. It wakes up the farmer.*
> • *Here is the farmer with a bucket of milk. He milked the cow.*
> • *Here are the farmer's children. His daughter is feeding the chickens. His son is collecting eggs from the hen's nest.*
> • *Here is the farmer's wife. She is feeding the pigs.*

Remove the storyboard pieces and allow children to replace each piece as they retell the story.

Storyboards

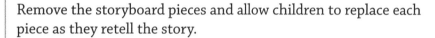

Section Three
Animals on the Farm

"Old MacDonald's Farm" Storyboard After singing "Old MacDonald Had a Farm," retell the story using the storyboard pieces on pages 105–109. You may choose to use the following teacher script to present the story:

Today we are going to sing a song about the animals on a farm. But before we begin, I want to be sure we all know how to make animal sounds. I will hold up a storyboard piece of one of Old MacDonald's animals. Then I will say the name of the animal. If you know the sound it makes, then make the sound! (Teacher says the name of a variety of animals on the farm, and children respond by making the sound of the animal.) *Now let's sing the song "Old MacDonald Had a Farm." I will give some of you a storyboard animal to hold. When we mention the animal you are holding, come and place it on the storyboard.*

Remove the storyboard pieces and allow children to replace each piece as they retell the story.

Section Four
Things That Grow on the Farm

"Harvest Time!" Storyboard Use the colorful storyboard pieces on pages 145 and 147 to follow up your presentation of the story "Harvest Time!" You may choose to use the following teacher script to present the story:

A farmer and his helpers pick fruits and vegetables when they are ripe. We say they harvest the crops. Let's use our storyboard pieces to talk about some of the things picked at harvest time.

- *This is a tree. Apples grow on a tree.*
- *Many apple trees growing together are called an orchard.* (Continue discussing other fruits that grow on a tree.)
- *This is a field. Many different things grow in a field.*
- *This is corn. Corn grows in a field.* (Continue with other crops that grow in a field.)
- *This is a garden. Many farms have gardens where the family grows some of the food they eat.*

Remove the storyboard pieces and allow children to replace each piece as they retell the story.

Storyboards

"The Apple's Adventure" Storyboard Use the storyboard pieces on pages 179 and 181 to follow up your presentation of the story "The Apple's Adventure." You may choose to use the following teacher script to present the story:

Have any of you ever helped out in the garden? What kinds of things can we do to make a garden grow? (Discuss the various things one does in a garden: planting seeds, tending plants, watering, weeding, etc.) *Let's all take a look at the storyboard pieces. They will help us show how an apple grows.*

- *These are apple seeds. They grow into an apple tree.*
- *This tree has apple flowers. The flowers are where apples will grow.* (Continue with the stages of growth.)
- *This tree has ripe apples. The farmer is picking the apples.*
- *The apples have to leave the farm to reach us. The farmer is putting crates of apples on a truck.*
- *The truck brought the apples to the grocery store.*
- *These apples are in the grocery store.*

Remove the storyboard pieces and allow children to replace each piece as they retell the story.

Creating an Atmosphere

Create a delightful farm environment in your classroom. Make a bulletin board that displays farm-related pictures and information. Display children's projects on the bulletin board area. Use a bale of hay or a wheelbarrow to display books about a farm.

Make a Farm Bulletin Board

- Staple blue butcher paper to the board as a backing.
- Cut objects such as a barn, a tree, corn, clouds, and bales of hay from construction paper or butcher paper, depending upon the size of your bulletin board area. Add details with a marker.

Simple Steps to Show You How

glue edges down
and fold open

Barn

- Cut a large square of red paper for the barn. Draw the lower half of the closed door with a marker.
- Cut a roof from black paper. Cut a square loft door from red paper. Glue it to the center of the barn roof.
- Cut two rectangles from red paper for the top half of the barn door. Glue the outside edges down to form a hinge; fold doors open.

Horse

- Cut a rectangle of brown paper for the horse's head. Round the bottom edges. Cut two slits on either side for the ears and fold the center portion down to create the forelock. Add details with a marker.

Hay

- Use yellow paper to make hay bales. Add details with a marker.

Tree

- Cut a tree trunk from brown paper. Cut a treetop from green paper.

Corn

- Cut cornstalks from green paper. Use yellow paper to make oval-shaped ears of corn. Add details with a marker.

Apples

- Pin up children's Colorful Apples art projects (page 183).

1

Welcome to the Farm!

Children are presented
with an overview of the farm, including
people, places, animals, and crops.

Welcome to the Farm!

Are you here to see the farm today?

Put on your hat.

We'll start right away!

Let's take a walk.
I'll show you the sights.
There's plenty to see.
Look left and look right.

2

Here is my family.

You'll see what they do.

Here are our helpers.
They do lots of work, too.

There are many animals
for you to see.

We raise fruits and vegetables.
They look tasty to me!

There are many machines that you will see.
Join harvest time with my family!

After all the work is done,
there's time for us to have some fun!

The End

Note: Teachers will make copies
and cut them in half for minibooks.

Reproducible Story

Welcome to the Farm!

Are you here to see

the farm today?

Put on your hat.

We'll start right away!

1

Let's take a walk.

I'll show you the sights.

There's plenty to see.

Look left and look right.

2

Here is my family.

You'll see what they do.

3

Here are our
helpers.
They do lots
of work, too.

4

There are many animals
for you to see.

5

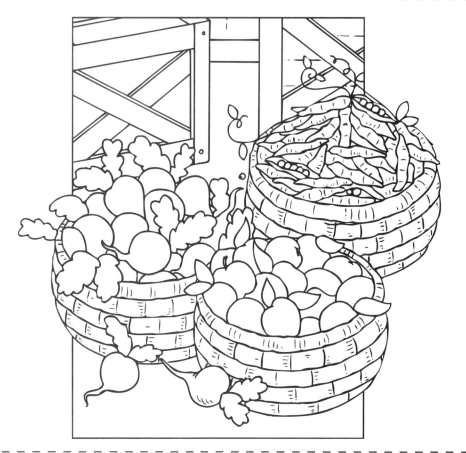

We raise fruits
and vegetables.
They look tasty
to me!

6

There are many
machines that
you will see.
Join harvest time
with my family!

7

After all the
work is done,
there's time for us
to have some fun!

8

The End

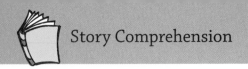

Note: Children color the pictures that were presented in Welcome to the Farm! circle-time story.

Name _____

Around the Farm

Color the things found on a farm.

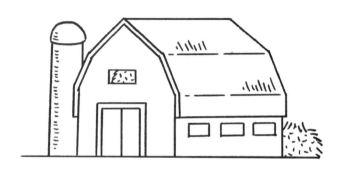

Note: See page 7 for suggestions on using the storyboard pieces on pages 29-33 for Welcome to the Farm!

Storyboard Pieces

Welcome to the Farm!

©2005 by Evan-Moor Corp.
All About the Farm • EMC 2402

Welcome to
the Farm!

©2005 by Evan-Moor Corp.
All About the Farm
EMC 2402

Welcome to the Farm!

©2005 by Evan-Moor Corp.
All About the Farm • EMC 2402

Welcome to the Farm!

©2005 by Evan-Moor Corp.
All About the Farm • EMC 2402

Welcome to the Farm!

©2005 by Evan-Moor Corp.
All About the Farm • EMC 2402

Welcome to the Farm!

©2005 by Evan-Moor Corp.
All About the Farm • EMC 2402

Welcome to the Farm!

©2005 by Evan-Moor Corp.
All About the Farm • EMC 2402

Welcome to the Farm!

©2005 by Evan-Moor Corp.
All About the Farm • EMC 2402

Welcome to the Farm!

©2005 by Evan-Moor Corp.
All About the Farm • EMC 2402

Welcome to the Farm!

Welcome to the Farm!

Welcome to the Farm!

Welcome to the Farm!

Welcome to the Farm!

Children create colorful self-portraits dressed for a day of work on the farm.

Materials

- page 36, reproduced on various skin-toned paper, one per child

- page 37, reproduced on white paper, one per child

- page 38, reproduced on light brown paper, one per child

- 6" x 12" (15 x 30 cm) blue construction paper, one per child

- paper scraps in a variety of colors (for eyes, nose, and mouth)

- strips of yarn in hair colors

- buttons, two per child

- scissors, crayons, and glue

Look at Me on the Farm

Preparation

1. Reproduce pages 36–38 on colored paper as shown, and cut out pieces for children if necessary.

2. Plan time to model the steps for this project and a completed Look at Me on the Farm self-portrait.

Steps to Follow

1. Give each child a piece of 6" x 12" (15 x 30 cm) blue construction paper, and have them fold and cut the overalls as shown below.

2. Children color the shirt and bib. Add hair and facial features, and assemble the pieces as shown above.

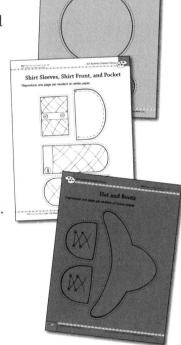

fold in half

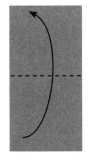

cut legs up to fold line

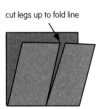

fold legs at knees

Note: Reproduce these patterns to use with Look at Me on the Farm art activity.

Face and Hands

Reproduce this page on skin-tone paper for each child.

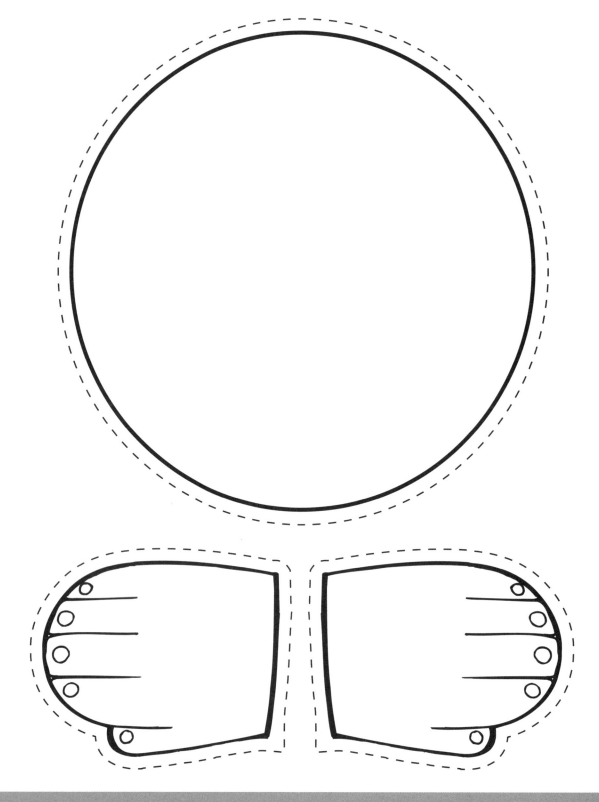

All About the Farm • EMC 2402 • ©2005 by Evan-Moor Corp.

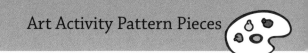
Shirt Sleeves, Shirt Front, and Pocket

Reproduce this page on white paper for each child.

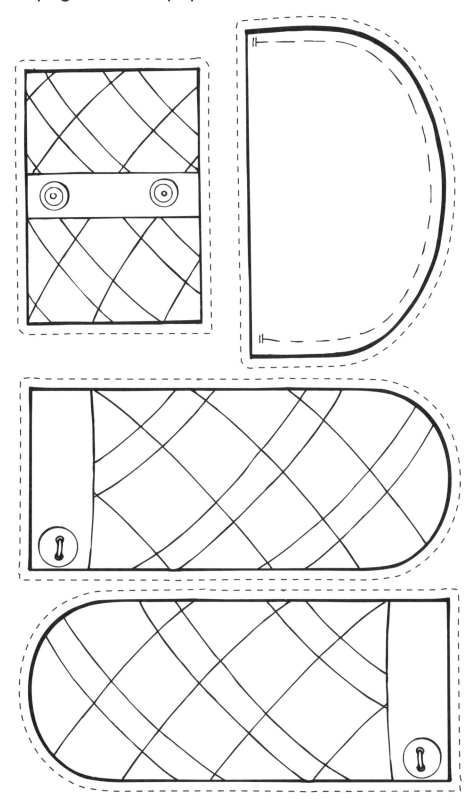

Note: Reproduce these patterns to use with Look at Me on the Farm art activity.

Hat and Boots

Reproduce this page on light brown paper for each child.

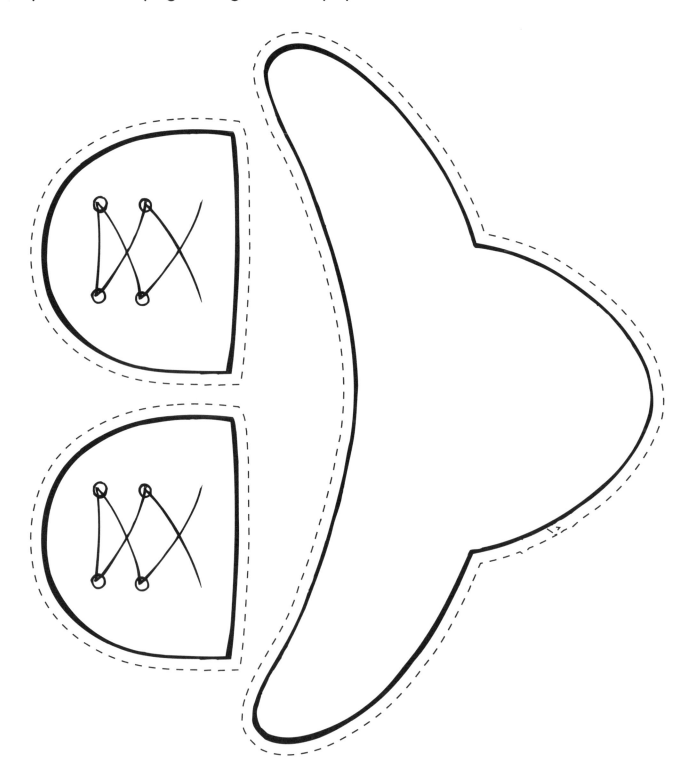

Note: Check for allergies before beginning any cooking activity.
An allergic reaction can occur through taste, smell, or contact with allergens.

Cooking Activity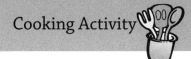

Children make easy "haystack" treats. Children will love the taste, and you will love the fact that they are simple and quick.

Haystacks

Materials

- 11.5 oz. (326 g) bag butterscotch morsels

- 2 cups (112 g) chow mein noodles

- waxed paper cut into 6" (15 cm) squares

- black marking pen

- large spoon

- large microwave-safe bowl

- microwave

- measuring cup

Preparation

1. Prepare a cooking center with all materials assembled.

2. Cut waxed paper into 6" (15 cm) squares for each child.

Steps to Follow

1. Children measure 1½ cups (258 g) of butterscotch morsels and pour them into a microwave-safe bowl. An adult heats the morsels for one minute. Children stir the morsels.

2. An adult heats the morsels again for 15 to 30 seconds. Children stir the morsels. Continue to heat and stir until the butterscotch is melted.

3. Children measure 2 cups of chow mein noodles and pour them into the bowl of melted butterscotch. Children stir the noodles until they are completely covered with butterscotch.

4. Once the mixture has cooled enough to be safe, each child spoons out a "haystack" onto a waxed paper square. Use a permanent-marking pen to write the name of each child on the paper. Allow the haystacks to set.

5. Enjoy this tasty treat!

Dear Parent(s) or Guardian(s),

Today we cooked in class. Your child helped prepare "Haystacks." Besides having fun cooking and eating, the children practiced these skills:

- listening to and following directions
- vocabulary development
- measurement
- using small motor skills

For our unit *The Farm*, we will send home a variety of new recipes. Each recipe will be one that your child has tried in class and is excited about. We hope you have an opportunity to try this recipe again with your child. Allowing your child to help you in the kitchen is a wonderful way to reinforce learning skills while creating family memories.

Haystacks

Materials

- 11.5 oz. (326 g) bag butterscotch morsels
- 2 cups (112 g) chow mein noodles
- cookie sheet
- waxed paper
- large spoon
- large microwave-safe bowl
- microwave

Steps to Follow

1. Have your child put the butterscotch chips in a microwave-safe bowl. Heat the butterscotch morsels in a microwave for no more than a minute at a time. Stir frequently. Heat until just melted.

2. Add the chow mein noodles to the melted butterscotch chips. Stir until all the noodles are covered.

3. Drop by teaspoons onto the waxed paper and let them cool approximately 20 minutes.

4. Enjoy!

This recipe makes about 4 dozen haystacks.

Note: Read the directions to children. Children help the farmer carry hay to the cow in the barn by coloring a path for him.

Language—Word Recognition ABC

Name _____

To the Barn

Help the farmer take the hay to the cow.
Color the boxes with the word **hay**.

hay	barn	pig	cow	chick
hay	pig	cow	chick	pig
hay	hay	cow	barn	chick
chick	hay	hay	hay	pig
cow	pig	duck	hay	barn
duck	pig	cow	hay	hay

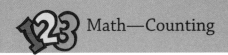

Name _____

Big Red Barn

Start at **2**. Connect the dots. Color the barn red.

1

20

2

19

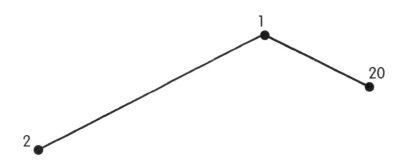

3 ●   ● 4   10 ●   ● 11   17 ●   ● 18

9 ●   ● 12

5 ●   ● 16

8 ●   ● 13

6 ●   ● 7   ● 14   ● 15

Note: Children count the items in each box and write the correct number to complete each sentence.

Math—Counting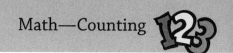

Name _____

On the Farm

| 1 | 2 | 3 | 4 | 5 | 6 | 7 | 8 | 9 | 10 |

Count. Write.

There are __4__ children.

There are _____ bales of hay.

There are _____ chicks.

There are _____ tractors.

There are _____ sheep.

There are _____ apples.

Peekaboo Barn Riddles

Creating the Center

1. Laminate and cut out pages 45 and 47.

2. Cut the barn doors on the lines indicated. Fold on the fold lines.

3. Store the barn and the farm characters in a sturdy folder or envelope.

Using the Center

1. Children may use the center in pairs or groups of three.

2. Children take the barn and the farm characters out of the envelope.

3. One child chooses a character and puts it "in the barn" as the others turn away or hide their eyes.

4. The child who hid the character makes up a riddle that reveals the character behind the barn doors. For example,

    I am very small.
    I am gray.
    I scurry quickly away and hide.
    I can be a pest.

5. The child who told the riddle calls on someone to give the answer (*a mouse*).

6. The child giving the correct answer gets to hide a character and make up a new riddle.

7. Children may play the riddle game until each character has been hidden.

Working in pairs, children hide a farm character in the barn and say a riddle for the others to solve.

Materials

- pages 45 and 47, laminated

- folder or envelope for storage

- scissors

- craft knife (adult use only)

Peekaboo Barn

fold

fold

Peekaboo Barn Riddles

Peekaboo Pictures

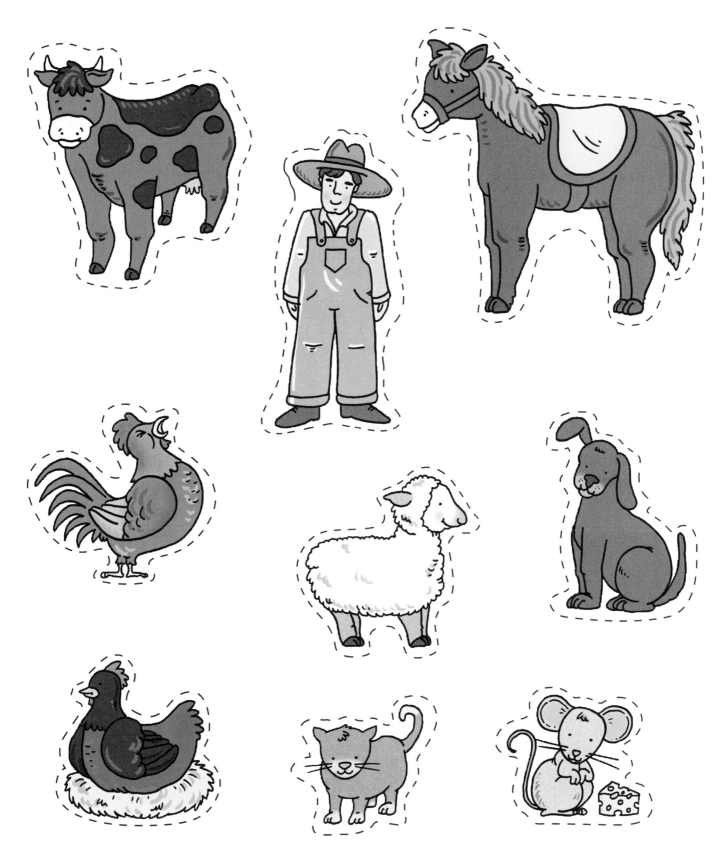

Peekaboo Barn Riddles

©2005 by Evan-Moor Corp.
All About the Farm • EMC 2402

Peekaboo Barn Riddles

©2005 by Evan-Moor Corp.
All About the Farm • EMC 2402

Peekaboo Barn Riddles

©2005 by Evan-Moor Corp.
All About the Farm
EMC 2402

Peekaboo Barn Riddles

©2005 by Evan-Moor Corp.
All About the Farm
EMC 2402

Peekaboo Barn Riddles

©2005 by Evan-Moor Corp.
All About the Farm
EMC 2402

Peekaboo Barn Riddles

©2005 by Evan-Moor Corp.
All About the Farm
EMC 2402

Peekaboo Barn Riddles

©2005 by Evan-Moor Corp.
All About the Farm
EMC 2402

Peekaboo Barn Riddles

©2005 by Evan-Moor Corp.
All About the Farm
EMC 2402

Peekaboo Barn Riddles

©2005 by Evan-Moor Corp.
All About the Farm
EMC 2402

Around the Farm Play Space

Children listen closely to see in which area of the farm they belong.

Materials

- page 50, reproduced, one tag per child
- card stock for signs
- marking pens
- chalk
- hole punch
- yarn

Preparation

1. Draw 4 large circles on the playground to represent each area: barn, corral, field, and garden.

2. Make a card stock sign for each area of the farm. Use both a picture and its name.

3. Make several copies of the tags on page 50. Color, laminate, and cut them out. Punch a hole in each and add a yarn tie. (Children will wear the tags around their necks.)

How to Play

1. One child stands in each designated farm space and holds up the appropriate sign.

2. The remaining children choose identification tags to wear. Then they stand in a line and wait for the teacher's directions.

3. The teacher tells each group which area of the farm they are to go to. For example, *All sheep go to the barn. All corn go to the field,* etc.

4. Once all the children are in their assigned place, the teacher calls out new directions. For example, *Corn to the garden. Sheep to the field,* etc.

5. Change sign holders after each game so everyone gets a chance to visit all the farm areas.

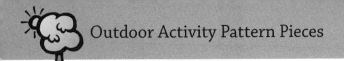

Note: Reproduce the tags below to use with Around the Farm Play Space outdoor activity.

Around the Farm Tags

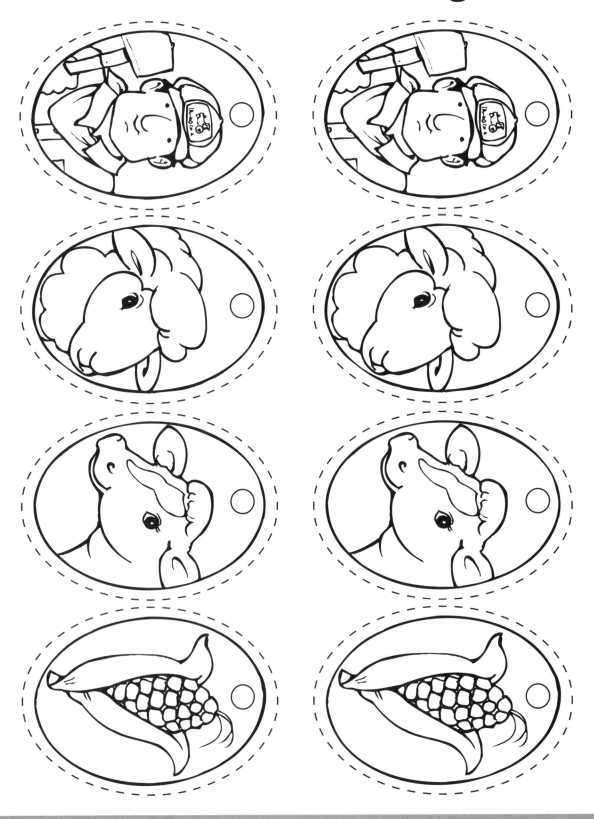

Note: Sing this song to the tune of "Did You Ever See a Lassie?" After children are familiar with the words, have them create actions for each verse.

Music/Dramatic Play Activity

If I Were a Farmer

If I were a farmer, a farmer, a farmer,

If I were a farmer, what would I do?

I'd sit on my tractor

And work in my fields.

If I were a farmer, that's what I'd do.

If I were a farmer, a farmer, a farmer,

If I were a farmer, what would I do?

I'd feed all my animals

And milk all my cows.

If I were a farmer, that's what I'd do.

If I were a farmer, a farmer, a farmer,

If I were a farmer, what would I do?

I'd harvest my fruit

And my vegetables, too.

If I were a farmer, that's what I'd do.

People on the Farm

2

Children are introduced to different people and family members who work on the farm. Children learn about some of the different jobs on a farm.

A Busy Day on the Farm

"Cock-a-doodle-do!" crows the rooster.

"It is time to wake up.

There is work to be done!"

1

Farmer Brown goes to the barn
and milks the cows. Now there
will be plenty of milk to drink.

Farmer Brown's children feed the chickens.
They gather the eggs.
Now there will be plenty of eggs to eat.

Mrs. Brown feeds the horses and the pigs.
There are many hungry animals on the farm!

After breakfast, the children
go to school. Mrs. Brown works
on the computer in the farmhouse.

Farmer Brown goes out to the
fields with his helpers.
They take care of the crops in the fields.

It has been a long day of work at home
and at school. Everyone is ready for
some fun. Farmer Brown plays the
banjo, and everyone sings.

All About the Farm • EMC 2402 • ©2005 by Evan-Moor Corp.

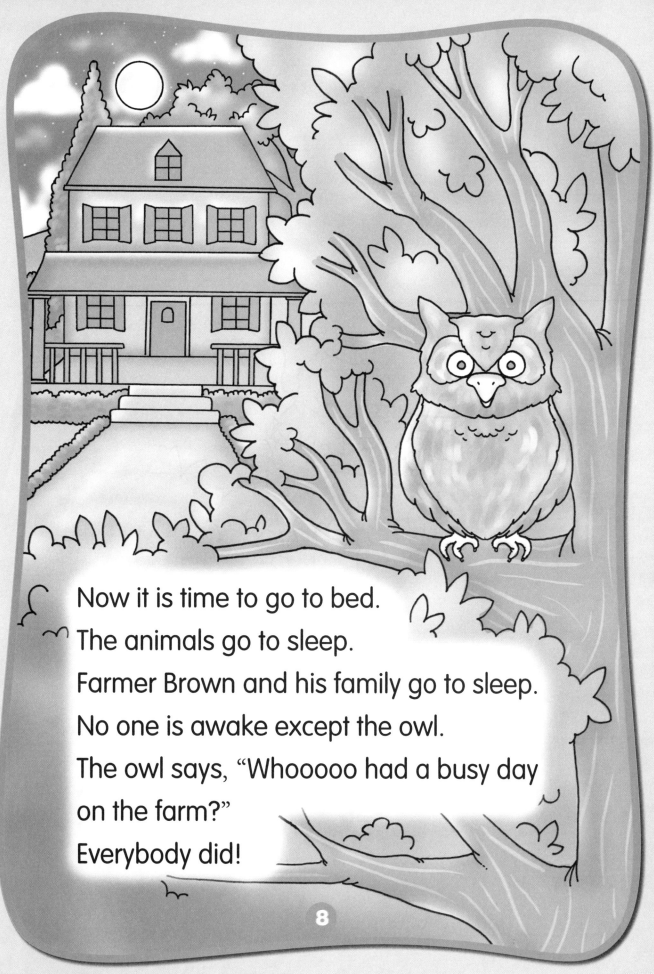

Now it is time to go to bed.

The animals go to sleep.

Farmer Brown and his family go to sleep.

No one is awake except the owl.

The owl says, "Whooooo had a busy day on the farm?"

Everybody did!

8

The End

Note: Teachers will make copies and cut them in half for minibooks.

Reproducible Story

A Busy Day on the Farm

"Cock-a-doodle-do!"

crows the rooster.

"It is time to wake up.

There is work to be done!"

1

Farmer Brown
goes to the barn
and milks the cows.
Now there will be
plenty of milk to drink.

2

Farmer Brown's
children feed
the chickens.
They gather the eggs.
Now there will be
plenty of eggs to eat.

3

Mrs. Brown
feeds the horses
and the pigs.
There are many
hungry animals
on the farm!

4

After breakfast,
the children go
to school.
Mrs. Brown works
on the computer in
the farmhouse.

5

Farmer Brown goes
out to the fields
with his helpers.
They take care of the
crops in the fields.

6

It has been a long
day of work at
home and at school.
Everyone is ready
for some fun.
Farmer Brown
plays the banjo,
and everyone sings.

7

Now it is time to go to bed. The animals go to sleep. Farmer Brown and his family go to sleep. No one is awake except the owl. The owl says, "Whooooo had a busy day on the farm?" Everybody did!

8

The End

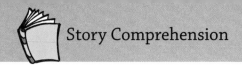

Note: Children draw a line from each person to the work he or she did on the farm.

Name _____

A Busy Day on the Farm

Draw a line to show who did each farm chore.

Note: See page 7 for suggestions on using the storyboard pieces on pages 69–73 for A Busy Day on the Farm.

Storyboard Pieces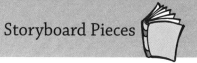

People on the Farm

People on
the Farm

People on the Farm

People on the Farm

People on the Farm

People on the Farm

People on the Farm   **73**

People on the Farm

©2005 by Evan-Moor Corp.
All About the Farm • EMC 2402

People on the Farm

©2005 by Evan-Moor Corp.
All About the Farm • EMC 2402

People on the Farm

©2005 by Evan-Moor Corp.
All About the Farm • EMC 2402

People on the Farm

©2005 by Evan-Moor Corp.
All About the Farm • EMC 2402

Feed the Chicken

Children create a delightful paper chicken that bobs its head and pecks the ground as children pretend to feed it!

Materials

- page 76, reproduced on sturdy white construction paper, one per child

- paper plates (about 7" [18 cm] diameter), one per child

- paper scraps or punched paper holes

- scissors

- glue or tape

- crayons

- hand-held vacuum (optional, but handy to clean up the "chicken feed" after the activity)

Steps to Follow

1. Children color and cut out page 76.

2. They fold a paper plate in half (younger children may need assistance with this step).

3. Then children use glue or tape to attach the chicken to the folded edge of the paper plate.

4. Children feed their chicken by sprinkling "chicken feed" (small scraps of paper or punched paper holes) on the floor and rocking it so it pecks the feed.

Extension

Ask children to name other animals on the farm and the kinds of food they might eat.

Note: Reproduce these patterns to use with Feed the Chicken art activity.

Feed the Chicken

Attach these pattern pieces
to a folded paper plate.

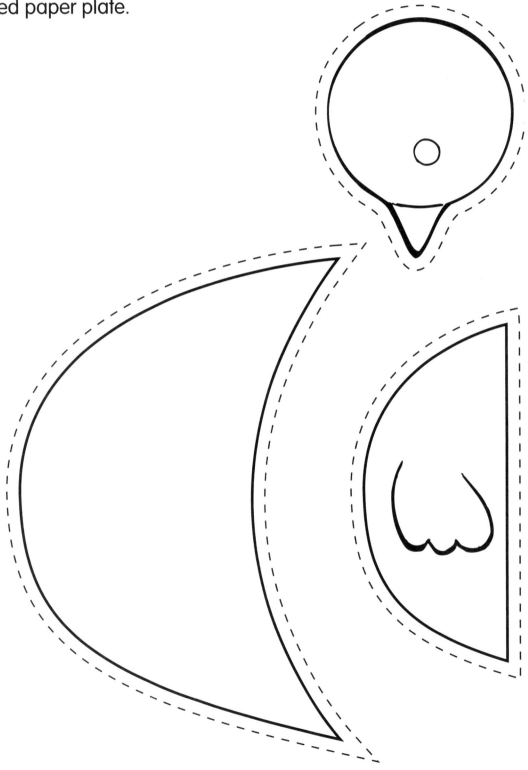

Note: Check for allergies before beginning any cooking activity.
An allergic reaction can occur through taste, smell, or contact with allergens.

Cooking Activity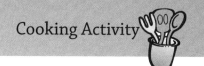

Children make a country breakfast for a real taste of farm living.

Materials

- page 81, reproduced, one per child
- ingredients:

  1 loaf of sliced white or wheat bread

  1 cup or 2 cubes softened butter (227 g)

  1 egg per child

  1 pint (473 mL) milk

  salt and pepper

- tools:

  large plastic bowl

  whisk or fork

  paper plates

  plastic forks

  dull-edged plastic knives

  frying pan or microwave container

  microwave or hot plate

  large serving spoon

  spatula

Farm Breakfast

Preparation

1. Prepare a cooking center with all materials assembled.

2. Plan on having some of the children make the placemats on page 81 while small groups rotate cooking with an adult.

Steps to Follow

Making Country Scrambled Eggs

1. Children crack an egg into a plastic bowl and stir it.

2. Children then add milk, salt, and pepper according to taste.

3. An adult pours the egg mixture into a buttered frying pan and cooks over medium heat.

Making Country Toast

1. Children place a slice of bread in a toaster and push down the lever on the toaster. Once the toast pops up, an adult places it on a plate.

2. Children spread butter on the toast with a dull-edged plastic knife.

3. Then children lay out their checkered placemats. An adult places the toast and eggs on plates and serves them to children.

Parent Letter

Dear Parent(s) or Guardian(s),

Today we cooked in class. Your child helped prepare a "Farm Breakfast." Besides having fun cooking and eating, the children practiced these skills:

- vocabulary development
- listening to and following directions
- using small motor skills
- patterning

For our unit *The Farm*, we will send home a variety of new recipes. Each recipe will be one that your child has tried in class. We hope you have an opportunity to try this recipe again with your child. Allowing your child to help you in the kitchen is a wonderful way to reinforce learning skills while creating family memories.

Farm Breakfast

Materials

- sliced white or wheat bread
- 1 Tbsp. softened butter per person (14 g)
- 1 to 2 eggs per person
- milk, salt, and pepper to taste
- large plastic bowl
- whisk or fork
- dull-edged plastic knife
- frying pan
- stove
- large serving spoon
- spatula

Making Country Scrambled Eggs and Toast

1. Crack one or two eggs for each person into a plastic bowl. Using a whisk or fork, beat the eggs until smooth. If you wish, give your child a chance to stir the eggs. Add milk, salt, and pepper according to taste.

2. Pour the egg mixture into a buttered frying pan or skillet and cook over medium heat while stirring. Cook the eggs until they are light and fluffy and all liquid evaporates.

3. Have children place the bread in a toaster at a medium or light setting and push down the lever of the toaster.

4. Place the toast carefully on a plate and allow children to use a dull-edged plastic knife to butter the toast.

5. Enjoy your meal!

Note: Review the tasks Farmer Brown did during the day. Children cut out and sequence the pictures.

Language—Sequencing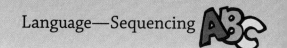

Name _____

Farmer Brown's Day

Cut. ✂ Glue. 🖊

Tell what happened—1, 2, 3.

1
2
3

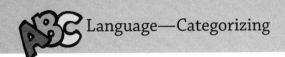 Language—Categorizing

Note: Ask children to name the animals and products on this page. Discuss other foods that come from a farm. Then they match the animal to the food it

Name _____

Where Does It Come From?

Draw a line to make a match.

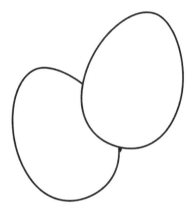

Note: Instruct children to color the squares in a pattern. If your children have limited experience with patterning, provide several examples that they may copy.

Math—Patterning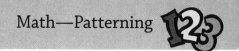

Checkered Placemat

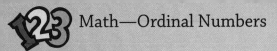
Math—Ordinal Numbers

Note: Review ordinal numbers from first through fifth. Read each direction aloud, giving children enough time to color each pair of overalls before reading the next direction.

Name _____

Count the Overalls

Color the 2nd pair of overalls   green.

Color the 5th pair of overalls   orange.

Color the 3rd pair of overalls   blue.

Color the 1st pair of overalls   purple.

Color the 4th pair of overalls   red.

This dress-up box provides imaginative role-playing fun for your little farmers!

Materials

- large box
- full-length mirror
- "farm-style" clothes:

  overalls

  men's shirts, especially flannel and checkered varieties

  straw hats

  old cotton dresses

  aprons

  work boots

  bandanas

Farmer Dress-up Box

Creating the Center

1. Gather together enough dress-up clothes to fill the box. Plan to have enough garments so that a small group of children can take part in this activity at the same time. Ask parents for donations and visit local thrift shops.

2. Create a dress-up center area. Place the box of clothing and a full-length mirror in the center so children can see themselves as they dress up.

Using the Center

1. Present the center to your whole class. Show the clothing pieces and ask children to name each piece, tell its color, and tell how it is used. Ask children to point out buttons, buttonholes, zippers, snaps, etc. Allow several children to demonstrate putting on the clothes for the class.

2. Ask children to categorize and count the pieces of clothing.

3. Explain that they may use the dress-up box during center time. Ask children to demonstrate how they should replace the clothing in the box after they are done playing.

Extension

Consider making over your playhouse area as a farmhouse. Allow children to use the dress-up clothes as part of a dramatic play in the playhouse area.

The Farmer in the Dell

Preparation

1. Teach children the words to "The Farmer in the Dell" (see page 85). Sing the first verse one phrase at a time and have students "echo" the phrase after you.

2. Then sing the whole verse, inviting children to join in when they are ready.

3. Repeat the process with each verse.

4. Plan to play in an outdoor space.

How to Play

1. Children go outside and form a circle, holding hands.

2. Select one child to be the "farmer." The farmer stands in the center of the circle.

3. Children walk or skip around in a circle as they sing the first verse. At the end of the verse, they stop, and the farmer picks someone to be the "wife." The wife joins the farmer in the center of the circle.

4. Children continue to walk in a circle and sing the song verses. For each song verse, one member in the center of the circle will invite another person to join them. For example,

    The child takes a nurse,
    The child takes a nurse,
    Hi-ho, the derry-o,
    The child takes a nurse.

5. After the "cheese" is chosen (10th verse), all other characters return to the circle as children sing, *The cheese stands alone,* etc.

   All About the Farm • EMC 2402 • ©2005 by Evan-Moor Corp.

The Farmer in the Dell

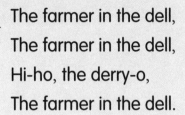

The farmer in the dell,
The farmer in the dell,
Hi-ho, the derry-o,
The farmer in the dell.

The farmer takes a wife,
The farmer takes a wife,
Hi-ho, the derry-o,
The farmer takes a wife.

The wife takes a child,
The wife takes a child,
Hi-ho, the derry-o,
The wife takes a child.

The child takes a nurse,
The child takes a nurse,
Hi-ho, the derry-o,
The child takes a nurse.

The nurse takes a cow,
The nurse takes a cow,
Hi-ho, the derry-o,
The nurse takes a cow.

The cow takes a dog,
The cow takes a dog,
Hi-ho, the derry-o,
The cow takes a dog.

The dog takes a cat,
The dog takes a cat,
Hi-ho, the derry-o,
The dog takes a cat.

The cat takes a rat,
The cat takes a rat,
Hi-ho, the derry-o,
The cat takes a rat.

The rat takes the cheese,
The rat takes the cheese,
Hi-ho, the derry-o,
The rat takes the cheese.

The cheese stands alone,
The cheese stands alone,
Hi-ho, the derry-o,
The cheese stands alone.

Down at the Barnyard

Preparation

Reproduce the song "Down at the Barnyard" on page 87 onto a transparency.

Steps to Follow

1. Display the transparency. Teach the song to the children.

2. As children look at the pictures on the transparency, talk about what the farmer, his family, and the workers are doing.

3. Invite children to act out unloading the truck and working in the garden.

4. Ask them to think of other kinds of work they might do on the farm. As a child names a type of work, have classmates act out the work.

   • They could feed the chickens.

   • The children could pick food in the garden.

   • Someone could drive the truck.

5. Give children drawing paper. Have them draw the farmer, someone in his family, or a farmworker at work. Then have them write or dictate a phrase or sentence naming the type of work. Provide time for children to share their pictures with the class. You may choose to bind the pages together to make a class book entitled "Down at the Barnyard."

   All About the Farm • EMC 2402 • ©2005 by Evan-Moor Corp.

Note: Sing this song to the tune of "Down by the Station."

Music/Dramatic Play Activity

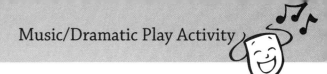

Down at the Barnyard

Down at the barnyard
Early in the morning,
See the busy farmer
Working in the sun.
See the farmer's helpers
Working all together,
Helping to get the day's work done.

Down at the farmhouse
Early in the morning,
See the busy farm wife
Working in the sun.
See the farmer's children
Working with their mother,
Helping to get the day's work done.

Animals on the Farm

Children are introduced to the animals on the farm. They learn to name the animals and to recognize their sounds. They discover some of the foods we eat that come from farm animals.

Old MacDonald Had a Farm

Old MacDonald had a farm, ee-i-ee-i-o!
And on his farm he had some chicks, ee-i-ee-i-o!
With a cluck-cluck here,
And a cluck-cluck there,
Here a cluck, there a cluck,
Everywhere a cluck-cluck.
Old MacDonald had a farm, ee-i-ee-i-o!

1

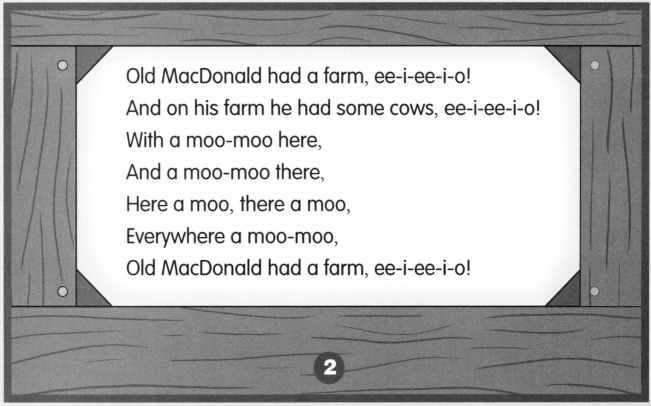

Old MacDonald had a farm, ee-i-ee-i-o!
And on his farm he had some cows, ee-i-ee-i-o!
With a moo-moo here,
And a moo-moo there,
Here a moo, there a moo,
Everywhere a moo-moo,
Old MacDonald had a farm, ee-i-ee-i-o!

2

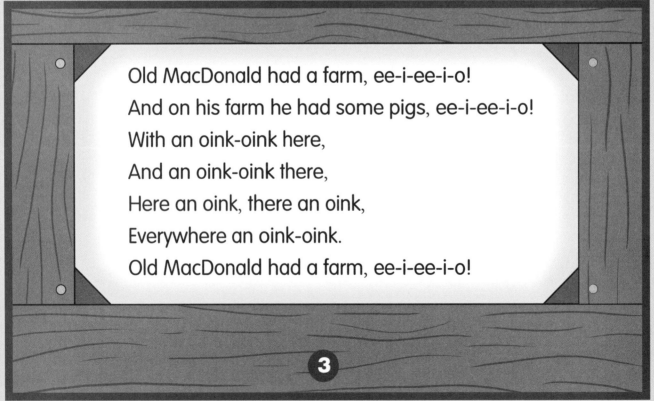

Old MacDonald had a farm, ee-i-ee-i-o!
And on his farm he had some pigs, ee-i-ee-i-o!
With an oink-oink here,
And an oink-oink there,
Here an oink, there an oink,
Everywhere an oink-oink.
Old MacDonald had a farm, ee-i-ee-i-o!

3

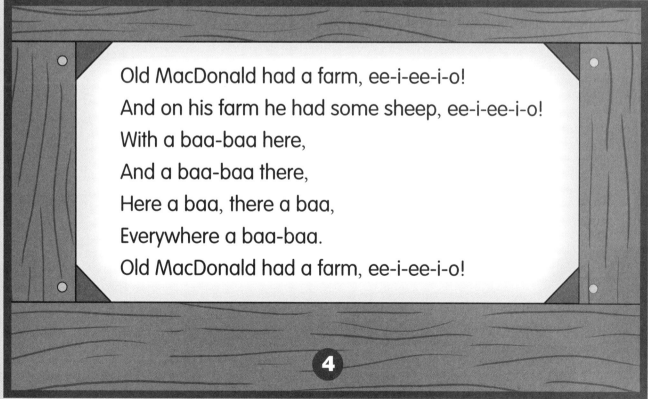

Old MacDonald had a farm, ee-i-ee-i-o!

And on his farm he had some sheep, ee-i-ee-i-o!

With a baa-baa here,

And a baa-baa there,

Here a baa, there a baa,

Everywhere a baa-baa.

Old MacDonald had a farm, ee-i-ee-i-o!

4

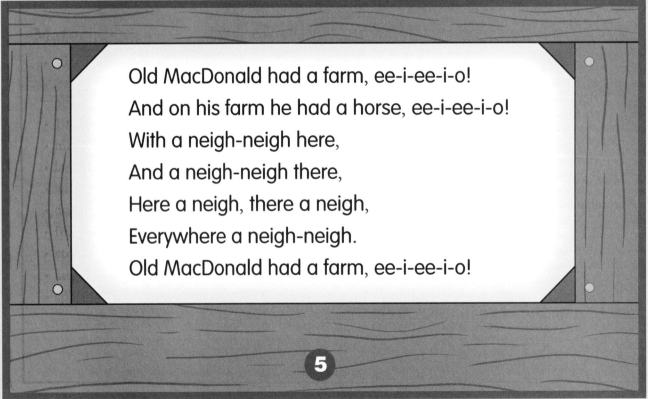

Old MacDonald had a farm, ee-i-ee-i-o!
And on his farm he had a horse, ee-i-ee-i-o!
With a neigh-neigh here,
And a neigh-neigh there,
Here a neigh, there a neigh,
Everywhere a neigh-neigh.
Old MacDonald had a farm, ee-i-ee-i-o!

5

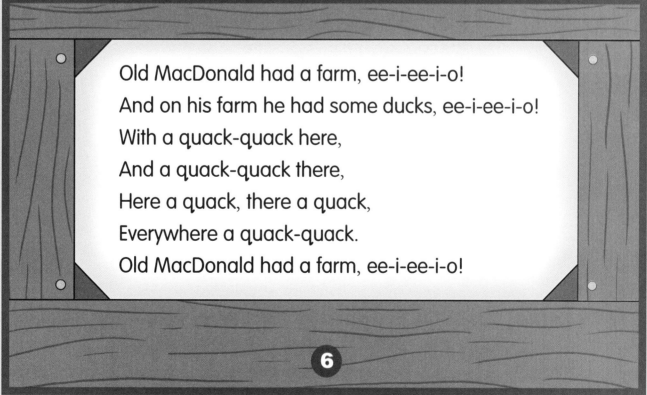

Old MacDonald had a farm, ee-i-ee-i-o!
And on his farm he had some ducks, ee-i-ee-i-o!
With a quack-quack here,
And a quack-quack there,
Here a quack, there a quack,
Everywhere a quack-quack.
Old MacDonald had a farm, ee-i-ee-i-o!

6

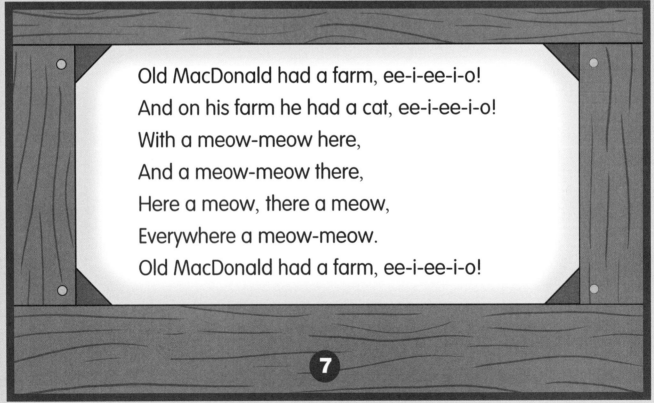

Old MacDonald had a farm, ee-i-ee-i-o!
And on his farm he had a cat, ee-i-ee-i-o!
With a meow-meow here,
And a meow-meow there,
Here a meow, there a meow,
Everywhere a meow-meow.
Old MacDonald had a farm, ee-i-ee-i-o!

7

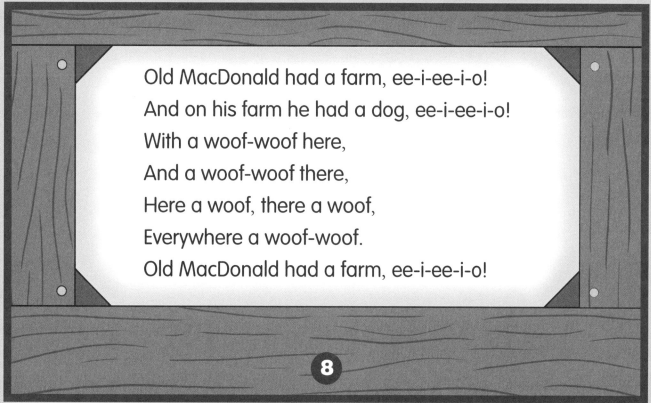

Old MacDonald had a farm, ee-i-ee-i-o!
And on his farm he had a dog, ee-i-ee-i-o!
With a woof-woof here,
And a woof-woof there,
Here a woof, there a woof,
Everywhere a woof-woof.
Old MacDonald had a farm, ee-i-ee-i-o!

8

The End

Note: Teachers will make copies
and cut them in half for minibooks.

Reproducible Story

Old MacDonald
Had a Farm

Old MacDonald had a farm,
        ee-i-ee-i-o!
And on his farm he had some chicks,
        ee-i-ee-i-o!

    With a cluck-cluck here,
    And a cluck-cluck there,
    Here a cluck, there a cluck,
    Everywhere a cluck-cluck.

Old MacDonald had a farm,
        ee-i-ee-i-o!

1

Old MacDonald had a farm,
ee-i-ee-i-o!
And on his farm he had some cows,
ee-i-ee-i-o!

With a moo-moo here,
And a moo-moo there,
Here a moo, there a moo,
Everywhere a moo-moo.

Old MacDonald had a farm,
ee-i-ee-i-o!

2

Old MacDonald had a farm,
ee-i-ee-i-o!
And on his farm he had some pigs,
ee-i-ee-i-o!

With an oink-oink here,
And an oink-oink there,
Here an oink, there an oink,
Everywhere an oink-oink.

Old MacDonald had a farm,
ee-i-ee-i-o!

3

Old MacDonald had a farm,
  ee-i-ee-i-o!
And on his farm he had some sheep,
  ee-i-ee-i-o!

  With a baa-baa here,
  And a baa-baa there,
  Here a baa, there a baa,
  Everywhere a baa-baa.

Old MacDonald had a farm,
  ee-i-ee-i-o!

4

Old MacDonald had a farm,
  ee-i-ee-i-o!
And on his farm he had a horse,
  ee-i-ee-i-o!

  With a neigh-neigh here,
  And a neigh-neigh there,
  Here a neigh, there a neigh,
  Everywhere a neigh-neigh.

Old MacDonald had a farm,
  ee-i-ee-i-o!

5

Old MacDonald had a farm,
ee-i-ee-i-o!
And on his farm he had some ducks,
ee-i-ee-i-o!

With a quack-quack here,
And a quack-quack there,
Here a quack, there a quack,
Everywhere a quack-quack.

Old MacDonald had a farm,
ee-i-ee-i-o!

6

Old MacDonald had a farm,
ee-i-ee-i-o!
And on his farm he had a cat,
ee-i-ee-i-o!

With a meow-meow here,
And a meow-meow there,
Here a meow, there a meow,
Everywhere a meow-meow.

Old MacDonald had a farm,
ee-i-ee-i-o!

7

Old MacDonald had a farm,
ee-i-ee-i-o!
And on his farm he had a dog,
ee-i-ee-i-o!

With a woof-woof here,
And a woof-woof there,
Here a woof, there a woof,
Everywhere a woof-woof.

Old MacDonald
had a farm,
ee-i-ee-i-o!

8

The End

Animals on the Farm

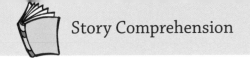

Story Comprehension

Note: Review the animals on Old MacDonald's farm. Children color only the animals that are on Old MacDonald's farm.

Name _____

Old MacDonald's Animals

Note: See page 8 for suggestions on using the storyboard pieces on pages 105–109 for Old MacDonald Had a Farm.

Storyboard Pieces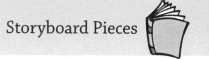

Animals on the Farm

Animals on the Farm

©2005 by Evan-Moor Corp.
All About the Farm • EMC 2402

Animals on the Farm

©2005 by Evan-Moor Corp.
All About the Farm • EMC 2402

Animals on the Farm

©2005 by Evan-Moor Corp.
All About the Farm • EMC 2402

Animals on the Farm   **107**

Animals on the Farm

Animals on the Farm

Animals on the Farm

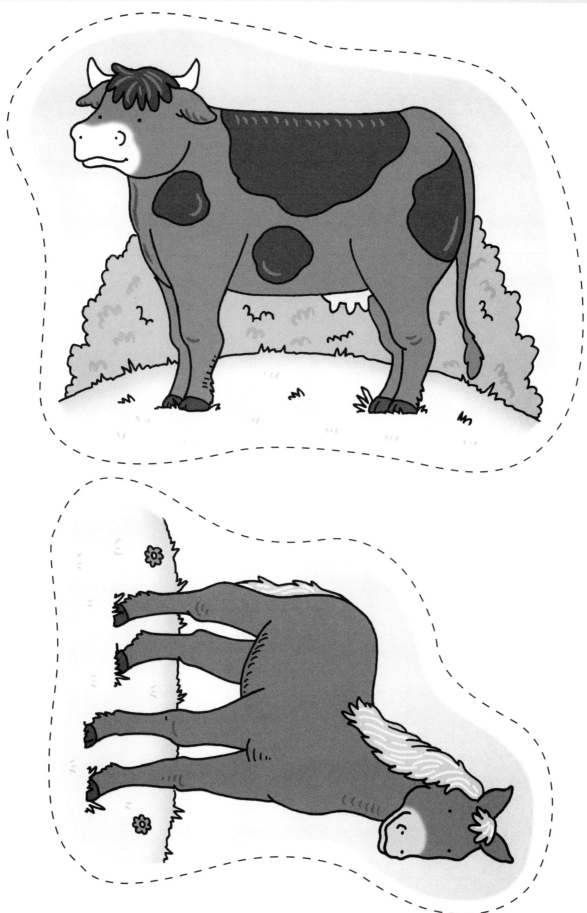

Animals on the Farm

Animals on the Farm

©2005 by Evan-Moor Corp.
All About the Farm • EMC 2402

Children practice cutting, coloring, and gluing to make a little hen's egg.

Little Hen's Egg

Preparation

1. Prepare an art center with all materials assembled.

2. Reproduce page 112 for each child.

3. Explain to children that female chickens are called *hens*. Tell children that hens are the animals on the farm that lay eggs. Explain that some chicken eggs grow up to be chicks, and others are used for food.

4. Plan time to model the steps for this project and a completed Little Hen's Egg.

Materials

- page 112, reproduced, one per child

- glue

- scissors

- crayons

Steps to Follow

1. Children color, cut out, and glue the chicken and egg picture on page 112.

2. As children work, share a book about eggs hatching. (Use resources from your local library or the Internet to gather pictures of chickens and eggs to share with the children.)

Extension

Discuss the differences between farm animals, pets, and wild animals. Give children drawing paper that has been folded in thirds. Ask them to draw a farm animal in one section, a pet animal in one section, and a wild animal in the last section.

glue

fold

Note: Check for allergies before beginning any cooking activity.
An allergic reaction can occur through taste, smell, or contact with allergens.

Cooking Activity
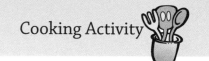

Children learn about dairy products while enjoying treats from the farm.

Materials

- assorted pictures of dairy products from magazines, newspapers, or books.

- small paper plates, plastic spoons for tasting

- ice cream (2 scoops per child)

- milk (¼ cup [60 mL] per child)

- chocolate syrup (1 Tbsp. [15 mL] per child)

- paper or plastic cups

- napkins

- large spoon

- ice-cream scoop

- blender

- drinking straws

Chocolate Cow Milkshakes

Preparation

1. Share the pictures of dairy products. Discuss all the different foods children eat that are made with milk products.

2. Glue the pictures of dairy products on a chart and label them. Display the chart, giving children the opportunity to read environmental print.

3. Because of the size of most electric blenders, you will probably make milkshakes for 4 or 5 children at a time. (Note: If you don't have a helper to supervise the shake-making, have the class complete the drawing part of the extension activity while you make the shakes with small groups.)

Steps to Follow

1. Children help scoop the ice cream into the blender.

2. Then they add chocolate syrup and pour the milk into the blender.

3. An adult turns the blender on and blends the milkshake until it looks smooth and creamy.

4. An adult pours the milkshake into small cups, places a straw in each cup, and serves each child a Chocolate Cow Milkshake.

Extensions

Provide children with drawing materials and ask them to draw a picture of a food that is made with milk. Encourage children to write or dictate details about their pictures.

Dear Parent(s) or Guardian(s),

Today we tasted things that are made from milk. Then your child helped prepare a "Chocolate Cow Milkshake." Besides having fun cooking and eating, the children practiced these skills:

- vocabulary and concept development
- listening to and following directions

For our unit *The Farm*, we will send home a variety of new recipes. Each recipe will be one that your child has tried in class and is excited about. We hope you have an opportunity to try this recipe again with your child. Allowing your child to help you in the kitchen is a wonderful way to reinforce learning skills while creating family memories.

Chocolate Cow Milkshake

Materials

- chocolate ice cream (2 scoops per shake)
- milk (¼ cup [60 mL] per shake)
- chocolate syrup (1 Tbsp. [15 mL] per shake)
- paper or plastic cups
- napkins
- large spoon
- ice-cream scoop
- blender
- drinking straws

Steps to Follow

1. Ask your child to help scoop the ice cream into the blender. Use two small scoops of ice cream, one Tbsp. (15 mL) chocolate syrup, and ¼ cup (60 mL) of milk per shake.

2. Allow your child push the button on the blender. An adult should stir the milkshake mixture if needed.

3. Continue to blend the milkshake until it looks smooth and creamy.

4. Pour the milkshake into small cups and serve with drinking straws.

5. Enjoy!

Note: Children determine which animals can usually be found on a farm and which ones are not farm animals.

Language—Categorizing

Name _____

Where Will You See Me?

Color. Cut.

Glue the animals in the correct place.

On the farm

glue	glue	glue

Not on the farm

glue	glue	glue

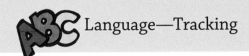

Name _____

Where Is My Mother?

Match each baby to its mother.

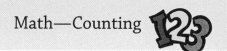

Note: Children count the number of animals in each row and write the number in the space provided. At the bottom of the page, they circle the animal with the most and the least.

Name _____

How Many?

| 1 | 2 | 3 | 4 | 5 | 6 | 7 | 8 | 9 | 10 |

Count. Write how many.

	_____ dogs
	_____ sheep
	_____ pigs
	_____ hens
	_____ cats

Which has the most?

Which has the least?

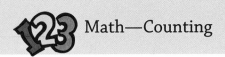

Note: Children count each hen's chicks and write the number in the box. At the bottom of the page, they circle the hen with the most chicks.

Name _____

How Many Chicks?

Count the chicks. Write the number.

3

Circle the hen with the most chicks.

Children put colorful eggs into an egg carton to create a pattern.

Materials

- page 120, reproduced, one per child

- page 121, laminated

- plastic eggs or individually laminated construction-paper eggs: 5 blue, 3 red, 2 green, 4 yellow, 4 purple

- basket for eggs

- 3 egg cartons

- two-sided tape

- crayons

- a sturdy box with a lid

Patterning Eggs

Creating the Center

1. Laminate and cut apart the patterning cards on page 121.

2. Tape one patterning card inside the lid of each egg carton.

3. Place the eggs in the basket.

4. Set out the egg cartons with the patterning tasks.

5. Then set out the patterning record forms and crayons.

Using the Center

1. Children choose an egg carton.

2. Then they take the eggs from the basket and use them to make the same pattern shown on the lid of the carton.

3. Then children use crayons to color the pattern on the record form.

4. Then children make and color the patterns shown on the other two egg cartons.

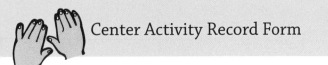

Name _____

I Can Make Patterns

Color to show the egg patterns you made.

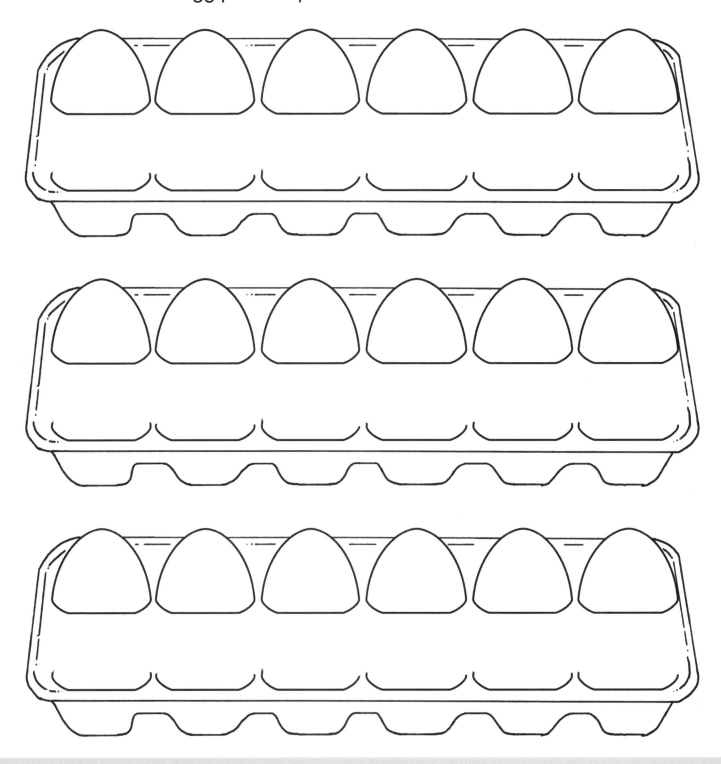

Patterning Eggs

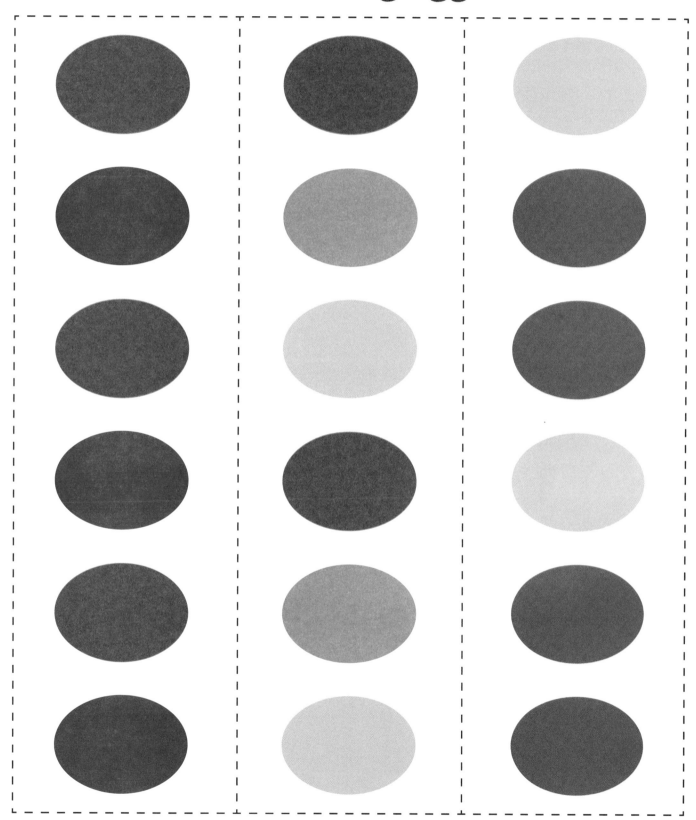

Patterning Eggs

©2005 by Evan-Moor Corp.
All About the Farm • EMC 2402

Patterning Eggs

©2005 by Evan-Moor Corp.
All About the Farm • EMC 2402

Patterning Eggs

©2005 by Evan-Moor Corp.
All About the Farm • EMC 2402

Farm Animals

Preparation

1. Reproduce the patterns at the bottom of the page to use as name tags for this outdoor game.

2. Have children color the animal tags.

3. Laminate and punch a hole in each tag. Add yarn to make the tag into a necklace.

How to Play

1. Children wear an animal name tag.

2. They sit in a large circle on the playground or a grassy area and follow the teacher's directions. (See suggestions below.)

   - *All cows, stand up and moo, etc.*
   - *All animals with four legs, stand up, etc.*
   - *All animals with feathers, stand up, etc.*
   - *Animals with the same covering (fur, feathers, scales, etc.), stand up.*

duck   chicken   horse

sheep   cow   pig

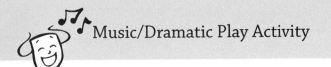

Note: Sing this song to the tune of "The Wheels on the Bus."

Animal Sounds Song

The **animals** on the farm all
  Make a noise,
  Make a noise,
  Make a noise.
The animals on the farm all
  Make a noise.
We can do it, too!

The **horse** on the farm goes
  Neigh, neigh, neigh,
  Neigh, neigh, neigh,
  Neigh, neigh, neigh.
The horse on the farm goes
  Neigh, neigh, neigh.
We can do it, too!

The **chicken** on the farm goes
  Cluck, cluck, cluck,
  Cluck, cluck, cluck,
  Cluck, cluck, cluck.
The chicken on the farm goes
  Cluck, cluck, cluck.
We can do it, too!

The **pig** on the farm goes
  Oink, oink, oink,
  Oink, oink, oink,
  Oink, oink, oink.
The pig on the farm goes
  Oink, oink, oink.
We can do it, too!

The **rooster** on the farm goes
  Cock-a-doodle-doo,
  Cock-a-doodle-doo,
  Cock-a-doodle-doo.
The rooster on the farm goes
  Cock-a-doodle-doo.
We can do it, too!

The **sheep** on the farm goes
  Baa, baa, baa,
  Baa, baa, baa,
  Baa, baa, baa.
The sheep on the farm goes
  Baa, baa, baa.
We can do it, too!

The **duck** on the farm goes
  Quack, quack, quack,
  Quack, quack, quack,
  Quack, quack, quack.
The duck on the farm goes
  Quack, quack, quack.
We can do it, too!

The **cow** on the farm goes
  Moo, moo, moo,
  Moo, moo, moo,
  Moo, moo, moo.
The cow on the farm goes
  Moo, moo, moo.
We can do it, too!

Five Little Lambs Finger Puppets

Steps to Follow

1. Children color and cut out the finger puppets on page 127.

2. Model how to tape the edges of the puppets.

3. Once the finger puppets are prepared, have children sit in a circle with their puppets in front of them on the floor in order from one to five.

4. Read aloud the poem on page 126. As you read the poem a second time, ask children to place a finger puppet on their fingers each time a little lamb is added in the poem.

   You say:

   One little lamb with nothing to do...

   and children place the first finger puppet on their thumbs and hold up their hands.

   Then you say:

   Along came another one, and then there were two...

   and children place the second finger puppet on their index fingers and hold up their hands.

5. Repeat until the poem is complete and children are wearing all five finger puppets.

Materials

- page 127, reproduced for each child

- crayons

- scissors

- tape

Five Little Lambs

One little lamb with nothing to do,
Along came another one,
And then there were two.

Two little lambs standing under a tree,
Along came another one,
And then there were three.

Three little lambs by the barn door,
Along came another one,
And then there were four.

Four little lambs by a beehive,
Along came another one,
And then there were five!

Five little lambs are happy to say
That you learned to count to five today!
One, two, three, four, five little lambs

Say "Good-bye!"

Note: Reproduce these patterns to use with Five Little Lambs finger play.

Five Little Lambs Finger Puppets

Cut out the lambs.

Tape the edge.

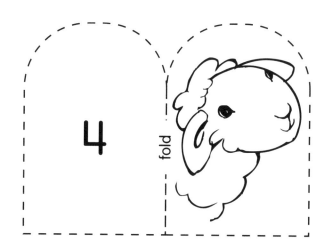

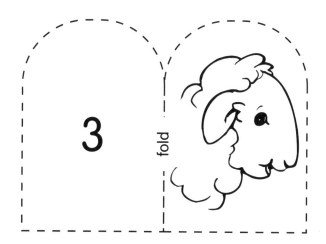

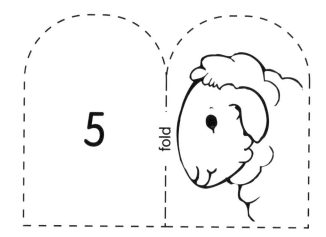

4

Things That Grow on the Farm

Children learn about some of the fruits and vegetables grown on a farm.

Harvest Time!

Harvest time, it's harvest time!

Oh, what do we pick at harvest time?

Pick the apples 1, 2, 3.

They'll taste good to you and me.

It's happy harvest time!

1

Harvest time, it's harvest time!

Oh, what do we pick at harvest time?

Pick the strawberries 1, 2, 3.

They'll taste good to you and me.

It's happy harvest time!

2

Harvest time, it's harvest time!

Oh, what do we pick at harvest time?

Pick the watermelons 1, 2, 3.

They'll taste good to you and me.

It's happy harvest time!

3

Harvest time, it's harvest time!

Oh, what do we pick at harvest time?

Pick the carrots 1, 2, 3.

They'll taste good to you and me.

It's happy harvest time!

4

Harvest time, it's harvest time!

Oh, what do we pick at harvest time?

Pick the corn 1, 2, 3.

They'll taste good to you and me.

It's happy harvest time!

5

Harvest time, it's harvest time!

Oh, what do we pick at harvest time?

Pick the potatoes 1, 2, 3.

They'll taste good to you and me.

It's happy harvest time!

6

Harvest time, it's harvest time!

Oh, what do we pick at harvest time?

Pick the beans 1, 2, 3.

They'll taste good to you and me.

It's happy harvest time!

Harvest time, it's harvest time!

Oh, what do I pick at harvest time?

Squash and tomatoes 1, 2, 3.

Food from my garden tastes good to me.

It's happy harvest time!

The End

Harvest Time!

Harvest time,

it's harvest time!

Oh, what do we pick

at harvest time?

Pick the apples 1, 2, 3.

They'll taste good

to you and me.

It's happy harvest time!

1

Reproducible Story

Harvest time,
it's harvest time!
Oh, what do we pick
at harvest time?
Pick the
strawberries 1, 2, 3.
They'll taste good
to you and me.
It's happy harvest time!

2

Harvest time,
it's harvest time!
Oh, what do we pick
at harvest time?
Pick the
watermelons 1, 2, 3.
They'll taste good
to you and me.
It's happy harvest time!

3

Harvest time,

it's harvest time!

Oh, what do we pick

at harvest time?

Pick the carrots 1, 2, 3.

They'll taste good

to you and me.

It's happy harvest time!

4

Harvest time,

it's harvest time!

Oh, what do we pick

at harvest time?

Pick the corn 1, 2, 3.

They'll taste good

to you and me.

It's happy harvest time!

5

Harvest time,

it's harvest time!

Oh, what do we pick

at harvest time?

Pick the potatoes 1, 2, 3.

They'll taste good

to you and me.

It's happy harvest time!

6

Harvest time,

it's harvest time!

Oh, what do we pick

at harvest time?

Pick the beans 1, 2, 3.

They'll taste good

to you and me.

It's happy harvest time!

7

Harvest time,

it's harvest time!

Oh, what do I pick

at harvest time?

Squash and

tomatoes 1, 2, 3.

Food from my garden

tastes good to me.

It's happy harvest time!

8

The End

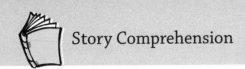
Note: Review the fruits and vegetables harvested in the story. Children find and color those fruits and vegetables.

Name _____

Help the Farmer at Harvest Time

Color the fruits and vegetables that the farmer picked.

Note: See page 8 for suggestions on using the storyboard pieces on pages 145 and 147 for Harvest Time!

Storyboard Pieces

**Things That Grow
on the Farm**

©2005 by Evan-Moor Corp.
All About the Farm • EMC 2402

**Things That Grow
on the Farm**

©2005 by Evan-Moor Corp.
All About the Farm • EMC 2402

**Things That Grow
on the Farm**

©2005 by Evan-Moor Corp.
All About the Farm • EMC 2402

**Things That Grow
on the Farm**

©2005 by Evan-Moor Corp.
All About the Farm • EMC 2402

**Things That Grow
on the Farm**

©2005 by Evan-Moor Corp.
All About the Farm • EMC 2402

**Things That Grow
on the Farm**

©2005 by Evan-Moor Corp.
All About the Farm • EMC 2402

All About the Farm • EMC 2402 • ©2005 by Evan-Moor Corp.

Things That Grow
on the Farm

©2005 by Evan-Moor Corp.
All About the Farm • EMC 2402

Things That Grow
on the Farm

©2005 by Evan-Moor Corp.
All About the Farm • EMC 2402

Things That Grow
on the Farm

©2005 by Evan-Moor Corp.
All About the Farm • EMC 2402

Things That Grow
on the Farm

©2005 by Evan-Moor Corp.
All About the Farm • EMC 2402

Things That Grow
on the Farm

©2005 by Evan-Moor Corp.
All About the Farm • EMC 2402

Things That Grow
on the Farm

©2005 by Evan-Moor Corp.
All About the Farm • EMC 2402

Things That Grow
on the Farm

©2005 by Evan-Moor Corp.
All About the Farm • EMC 2402

Things That Grow
on the Farm

©2005 by Evan-Moor Corp.
All About the Farm • EMC 2402

Children paint large colorful baskets of fresh vegetables and fruits from the farm.

Materials

- paint station (easel, wall, or table)
- newspaper or oilcloth
- tempera paint (various colors)
- paintbrushes
- paint paper
- scissors
- brown butcher paper
- pushpins or stapler

Paint a Harvest

Preparation

1. Prepare an art center with all materials assembled.

2. Cover a paint center area with newspapers or oilcloth to catch spills. Plan in advance where paintings will be placed to dry.

3. Provide a display of fresh vegetables and fruits to inspire your young painters. (Try to find vegetables and fruits that have their leaves intact, such as carrots with leaves, corn with husks, peas in pods, etc.)

Steps to Follow

1. Children paint a picture of one or two of the vegetables or fruits. Explain that they are to make their vegetables or fruits large enough to fill the paper.

2. Once paintings are dry, ask children to share them with the class. Tell children to name and describe the vegetable(s) or fruit(s) they painted.

Extension

Use these colorful painted fruits and vegetables to make a bulletin board display. Cut a large crate from brown butcher paper. Add details with marking pens. Add a caption such as "Harvest Time" or "Fruits and Vegetables from the Farm." Have students cut out their paintings (write their name on the back). Pin them to the crate on the board. Tuck some inside the crate and stack others next to the crate.

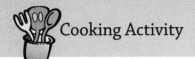 Cooking Activity

Note: Check for allergies before beginning any cooking activity. An allergic reaction can occur through taste, smell, or contact with allergens.

Fruit Salad

Children identify different fruits and combine them to make a tasty fruit salad.

Materials

- various fruits in season
- plastic cups or small bowls
- serving spoons
- plastic bowls for cut fruit
- paper towels
- 2 large cutting boards
- sharp knife (for adult use only)
- dull plastic knives for children to use
- plastic forks

Preparation

1. Prepare a cooking center with all materials assembled.
2. Set up two cutting boards, one for adult use and a second board so children can take turns slicing bananas or other soft fruits with a dull plastic knife.

Steps to Follow

1. Show children the whole fruits and ask them to name each one. Talk about how each type of fruit grows (on a tree, low to the ground, etc.).
2. An adult should cut the fruit into small pieces. Place each kind of fruit in its own bowl.
3. Call children one at a time to select the combination of fruits they would like in their fruit salad. They spoon a few pieces of each kind of fruit into their plastic cup or bowl.
4. Enjoy!

Extension

Add frozen yogurt, ice cream, or whipped cream for a special taste treat.

Dear Parent(s) or Guardian(s),

Today we cooked in class. Your child helped prepare fruit salad. Besides having fun cooking and eating, the children practiced these skills:

• listening to and following directions

• vocabulary and concept development

• using small motor skills

For our unit *The Farm,* we will send home a variety of new recipes. Each recipe will be one that your child has tried in class and is excited about. We hope you have an opportunity to try this recipe again with your child. Allowing your child to help you in the kitchen is a wonderful way to reinforce learning skills while creating family memories.

Fruit Salad

Materials

• various fruits in season

• plastic bowl for cut fruit

• large spoon

• paper towels

• cutting board

• sharp knife (for adult use only)

• dull plastic knife for child to use

• small bowl and fork

Steps to Follow

1. Show your child the various fruits you have selected for the fruit salad. Ask your child to name the fruits and then help decide what combination of fruits should go in the fruit salad.

2. Cut up the fruit and place in a bowl. Allow your child to slice bananas and other soft fruit with a dull plastic knife.

3. For a special fruit salad, add a bit of frozen yogurt, ice cream, or whipped cream.

4. Serve the fruit salad and enjoy!

Name _____

Yummy Fruit

Color.

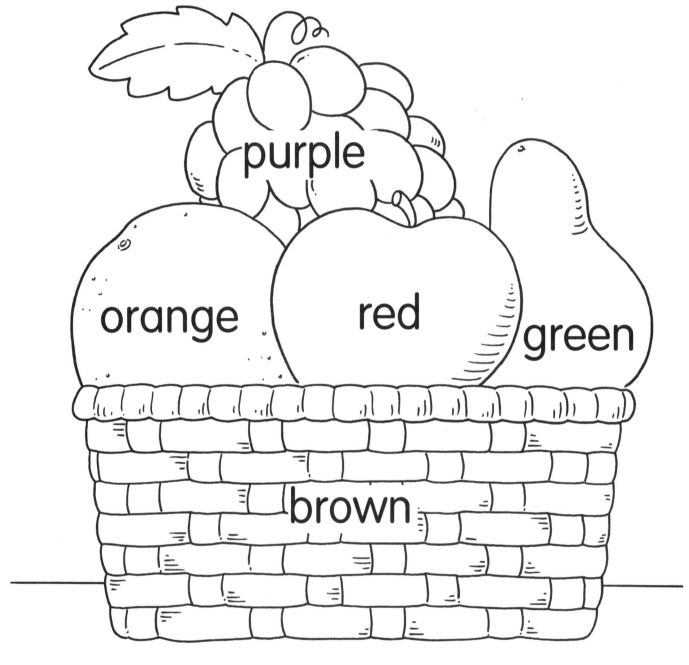

Note: Review the names of the pictures. Children listen to the beginning sound and color the pictures in each row that have the same beginning sound.

Language—Sound Recognition

Name _____

Listen for the Sound

Color the pictures in each row that begin with the same sound.

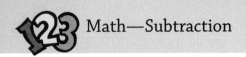
Note: Children count the number of items that do <u>not</u> have an **X** and write the correct number in the box.

Name _____

How Many Are Left?

Count. Write the number.

How many are left? | 4

How many are left?

How many are left?

How many are left?

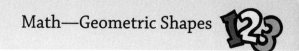

Note: Review color words with children. You may wish to display a chart with the colors and their names as a guide for young learners. Review the names of the geometric shapes. Children follow the chart to color the shapes below.

Name _____

Color the Shapes

Color.

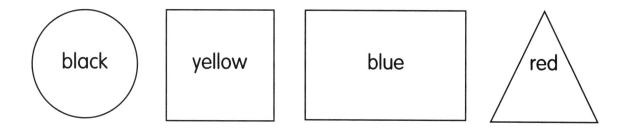

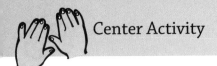

Note: This activity is not suitable for children under age three because of choking risk.

Sprouting Seeds

Preparation

1. Prepare a planting center. Laminate the center chart on page 157. Post the chart at the planting center. Place plastic cups, bean seeds (in a large plastic bowl), paper towels, and a source of water on a worktable.

2. Discuss the planting center with your class. Model the steps for placing seeds in the sprouting cups. Refer to the chart and point to each picture as you model what to do.

3. Reproduce pages 158 and 159 for each child.

Steps to Follow

1. Children print their name on a piece of masking tape and affix the masking tape to the side of a plastic cup. Assist children as needed.

2. Children visit the planting center in small groups.

3. They follow the steps on the chart to plant their seeds.

4. Children water the cups every day or two, making sure the paper towels remain moist.

5. Once the plants sprout and the seed leaves open, children examine them and talk about the parts they can see. Discuss the meaning of the following terms and relate them to what the children observe: *sprout, root, stem, leaves*.

6. Using pages 158 and 159, children put together a puzzle showing the parts of a plant.

Children plant seeds and watch them sprout.

Materials

- page 157, laminated
- pages 158 and 159, reproduced, one per child
- clear plastic cups, one per child
- dry beans, ten per child
- paper towels
- water
- black marking pen
- masking tape
- plastic bowl (for beans)
- pail for water
- cookie sheets
- scissors

Sprouting Seeds

Take: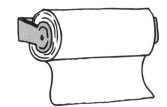

1

Wet a paper towel.

Squeeze it.

2

Put it in a cup.

3

Place seeds between the paper towel and the cup.

4

Place the cup in a sunny area.

Things That Grow on the Farm

Note: Reproduce this page to use with Sprouting Seeds center activit‍
Children cut out the pieces and glue them onto page 159.

Parts of a Plant

 Cut. Glue. Color.

leaf

flower

stem

roots

Note: Reproduce this page to use with Sprouting
Seeds center activity on page 158.

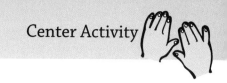

Name _____

Parts of a Plant

glue	glue
glue	glue

Upset the Fruit Basket!

Children run and change places with other fruits when they hear, "Upset the fruit basket!"

Preparation

1. Reproduce the fruit patterns at the bottom of the page (one tag per child) to use as name tags for this outdoor game.

2. Color, laminate, and cut out the tags.

3. Punch a hole and add a yarn tie to each tag.

4. Draw large X's in a circle on the playground. Draw an X for every child to stand on *except* one child, who will stand in the middle of the circle.

How to Play

1. Give one name tag to each child.

2. Select one child to stand in the center of the circle.

3. Call out the name of one of the "fruits." All children belonging to that group must change places with someone else in the same group.

4. As children run to a new spot, the child in the center tries to reach an empty spot. The child left with no place to go must stand in the center until the next fruit is called.

5. When the teacher calls out, *Upset the fruit basket!* everyone must change places. (Set some guidelines to minimize the chances of children bumping into each other.)

apple   orange   banana

pear   strawberry   grapes

This dramatic play activity gives children the chance to pretend to be their favorite vegetables. It may be presented as a play for parents or other visitors.

Materials

- large card stock squares, one per child
- crayons
- yarn
- scissors
- brown blanket
- straw hat
- basket
- watering can

Farmer Brown's Vegetable Garden

Steps to Follow

1. Children draw a picture of their favorite vegetable on a large square of card stock.

2. Label children's pictures. Laminate, punch holes, and string with yarn to form a necklace. Use this part of the activity as an opportunity to reinforce word recognition and oral language skills.

3. Place a brown blanket on the floor. Tell children that the blanket will be the dirt in the garden. Give each child the vegetable sign he or she created, and explain that the child will pretend to be that vegetable.

4. Select one child to play the part of the farmer. The farmer wears a hat and carries a watering can. The farmer makes up his or her own dialog while planting, watering, and harvesting the vegetables.

How to Play

1. Children crouch down into a ball and pretend to be the seed on the brown blanket. The farmer pats each one as if planting the seed in the dirt.

2. As the farmer "waters" them with the watering can, children begin to move toward a kneeling position and pretend to be a sprouting plant.

3. Finally, children sit tall on their knees and pretend to be a full-grown vegetable.

4. The farmer moves among the vegetables, carrying a basket and picking them (taking their necklaces and placing them in the basket).

From My Farm to Your House

This section focuses on one
farm crop (apples) from the time it is planted on the farm
until it is purchased and then eaten at home.

The Apple's Adventure

When you eat a crisp,
sweet, juicy apple today,
remember that it came from
a farm far away!

First grew a seed,
then a tree with a flower.
Then a tiny fruit grew
hour after hour.

When the fruit was ripe,
a farmer picked it for you.
Then it went many places;
here are just a few…

First, it went into a crate,
and then a truck or train.
It might have even traveled
on a ship or in a plane.

Then, it went to a warehouse,
and then to a store,
where workers put it in a bin
with many, many more.

Then, you bought it at the store,
and took it home with you.
And before you ate it,
there was one thing more to do…

You washed the fruit carefully
and put it on a plate.
And when you took a bite, you said,
"Yum! This tastes so great!"

 All About the Farm • EMC 2402 • ©2005 by Evan-Moor Corp.

So, if you eat a crisp,
sweet, juicy apple today,
remember that it came
from a farm far away!

The End

Note: Teachers will make copies and cut them in half for minibooks.

Reproducible Story

The Apple's Adventure

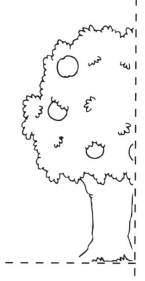

When you eat a crisp, sweet, juicy apple today, remember that it came from a farm far away!

1

Reproducible Story

First grew a seed,
then a tree with a flower.
Then a tiny fruit grew
hour after hour.

2

When the fruit
was ripe, a farmer
picked it for you.
Then it went many
places; here are
just a few…

3

All About the Farm • EMC 2402 • ©2005 by Evan-Moor Corp.

First, it went into
a crate, and then
a truck or train.
It might have even
traveled on a ship
or in a plane.

4

FARM FRES

Then, it went to
a warehouse, and
then to a store,
where workers
put it in a bin with
many, many more.

5

Then, you bought it at the store, and took it home with you. And before you ate it, there was one thing more to do…

6

You washed the fruit carefully and put it on a plate. And when you took a bite, you said, "Yum! This tastes so great!"

7

So, if you eat a crisp, sweet, juicy apple today, remember that it came from a farm far away!

8

The End

Story Comprehension

Note: Review the steps the apple passes through in the story. Children cut out the pictures at the bottom of the page and glue them in the correct order in the boxes.

Name _____

Apples!

Color.  Cut. Glue.

1	2	3
4	5	6

Note: See page 9 for suggestions on using the storyboard pieces on pages 179 and 181 for The Apple's Adventure.

Storyboard Pieces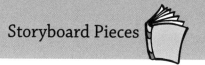

From My Farm
to Your House

©2005 by Evan-Moor Corp.
All About the Farm • EMC 2402

From My Farm
to Your House

©2005 by Evan-Moor Corp.
All About the Farm
EMC 2402

From My Farm
to Your House

©2005 by Evan-Moor Corp.
All About the Farm • EMC 2402

From My Farm
to Your House

©2005 by Evan-Moor Corp.
All About the Farm • EMC 2402

**From My Farm
to Your House**

©2005 by Evan-Moor Corp.
All About the Farm • EMC 2402

**From My Farm
to Your House**

©2005 by Evan-Moor Corp.
All About the Farm • EMC 2402

**From My Farm
to Your House**

©2005 by Evan-Moor Corp.
All About the Farm • EMC 2402

**From My Farm
to Your House**

©2005 by Evan-Moor Corp.
All About the Farm • EMC 2402

Colorful Apples

Children make delicious-looking red, yellow, or green apples.

Materials

- page 184, reproduced, one per child
- page 185, reproduced one per child
- red, yellow, and light green construction paper
- white construction paper
- crayons
- scissors
- glue
- apple seeds (optional)

Preparation

1. Prepare an art center with all materials assembled.

2. Reproduce page 184 on red, yellow, and light green construction paper. This will give you a variety of apples. Each child will choose one apple.

3. Reproduce page 185 on white construction paper for each child.

Steps to Follow

1. Children choose an apple color and then cut out the apple (page 184).

2. They color the other apple parts (page 185) and then cut them out.

3. Then children glue the apple parts to the construction paper apple.

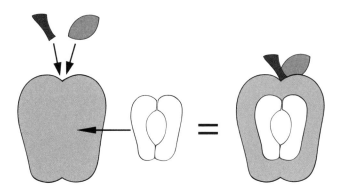

4. Children use crayons to draw (or glue real apple seeds) in the center of the apple.

Extension

Have children describe their apples. *I have a green apple. It has black seeds in the middle. Green apples taste good.*

Art Activity Pattern Piece

Note: Reproduce this pattern to use with Colorful Apples art activity.

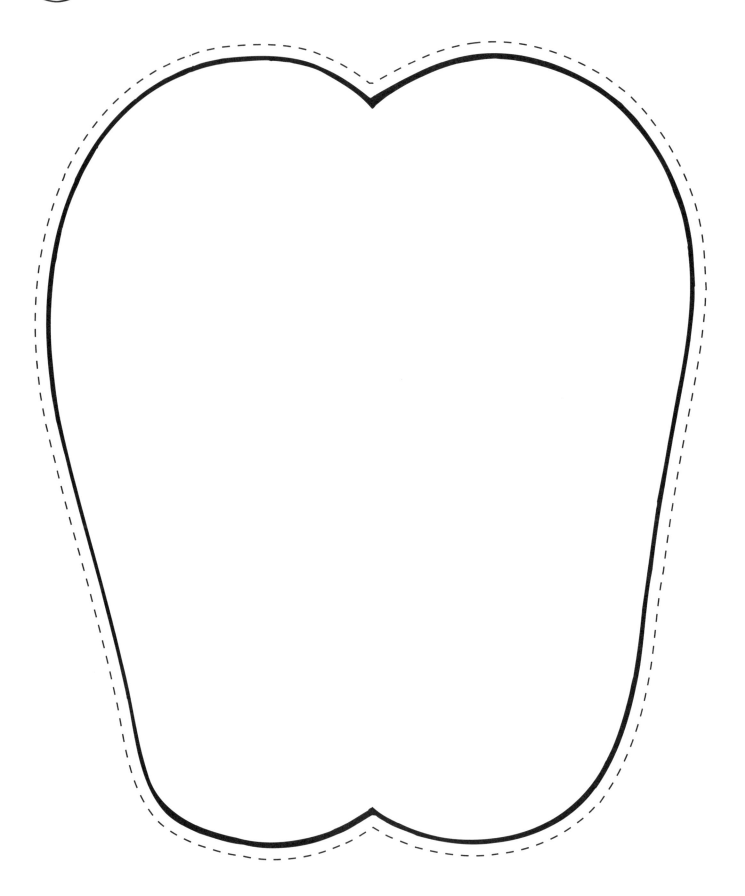

Note: Reproduce these patterns to use with Colorful Apples art activity.

Art Activity Pattern Pieces

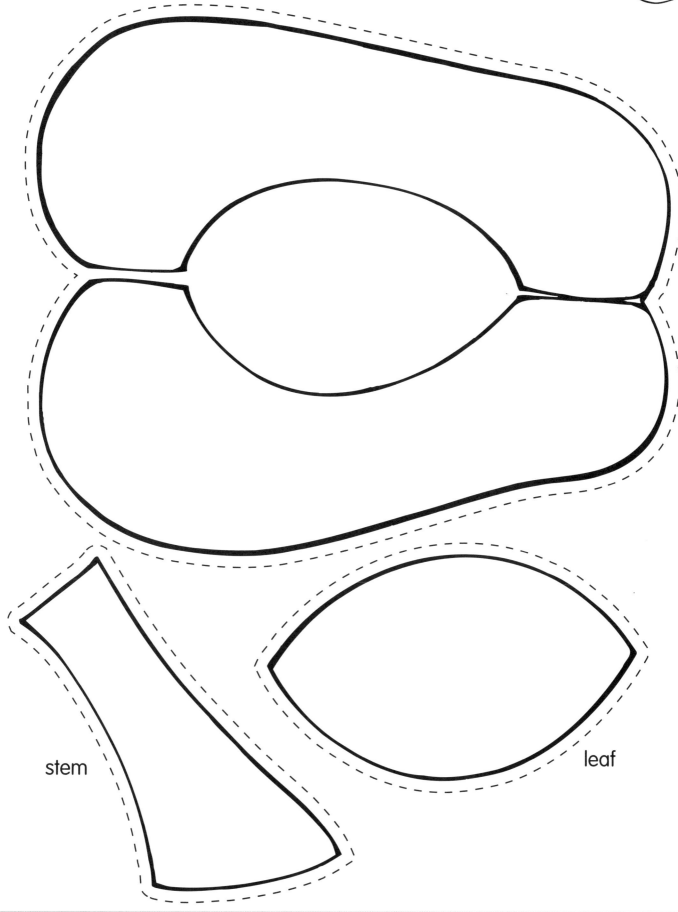

stem

leaf

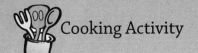

Note: Check for allergies before beginning any cooking activity. An allergic reaction can occur through taste, smell, or contact with allergens.

Children help turn apples into delicious applesauce.

Applesauce

Preparation

1. Prepare a cooking center containing all the materials needed to make the applesauce.

2. Cut apples into cubes.

Steps to Follow

1. Show children the ingredients and ask them to identify each one.

2. Call on children to assist in measuring and pouring the sugar and water into the pot. Then allow them to place the apple cubes in the pot.

3. Simmer the apples for 20 to 25 minutes. Stir occasionally. (It will require much less cooking time if you are using a microwave oven.) Add more water if needed.

4. While the applesauce is cooking, reread "The Apple's Adventure" to children.

5. Ask children to share stories about some of the things they have eaten that are made from apples or other fruits.

6. Once the applesauce has cooled, select one or more children to spoon it into cups and distribute it to classmates to eat.

Materials

- 2 pounds of tart cooking apples

- ½ to ⅔ cup (100 to 135 g) sugar (depends on the tartness of the apples)

- ½ cup (115 mL) water

- sharp knife (for adult use only)

- small plastic or paper cups

- plastic spoons

- large spoon

- paper towels

- cutting board

- hot plate or microwave oven (If you use a hot plate, tape off an area where children are not to enter during cooking.)

- pot or microwave container

- measuring cup

All About the Farm • EMC 2402 • ©2005 by Evan-Moor Corp.

Dear Parent(s) or Guardian(s),

Today we cooked in class. Your child helped prepare fresh applesauce. Besides having fun cooking and eating, the children practiced these skills:

- vocabulary and concept development
- listening to and following directions
- using small motor skills

For our unit *The Farm*, we will send home a variety of new recipes. Each recipe will be one that your child has tried in class and is excited about. We hope you have an opportunity to try this recipe again with your child. Allowing your child to help you in the kitchen is a wonderful way to reinforce learning skills while creating family memories.

Applesauce

Materials

- 2 pounds of tart cooking apples
- ½ to ⅔ cup (100 to 135 g) sugar (depends on the tartness of the apples)
- ½ cup (115 mL) water
- sharp knife (for adult use only)
- large spoon
- cutting board
- saucepan or microwave container
- measuring cup

Steps to Follow

1. Cut the apples into cubes at the center.

2. Allow your child to help measure the sugar and water to go into the pan and then place the apple cubes in the pan.

3. Simmer the apples for 20 to 25 minutes. Stir occasionally. (It will require much less cooking time if you are using a microwave oven.) Add more water if needed. While the applesauce is cooking, read the "Apple's Adventure" book your child brought home. Talk about some of the things your family eats that are made from apples or other fruits.

4. Once the applesauce has cooled, spoon some into a dish and enjoy!

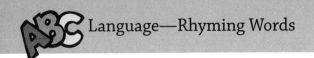 Language—Rhyming Words

Name _____

Apple Tree Rhymes

Cut. Glue.

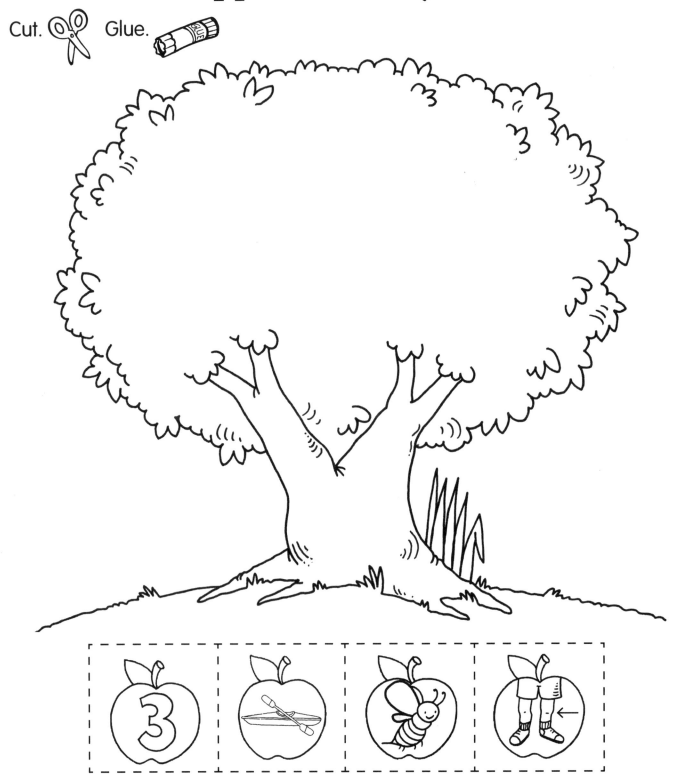

From My Farm to Your House   All About the Farm • EMC 2402 • ©2005 by Evan-Moor Corp.

Name _____

A Snack in a Tree

Start at **1**. Connect the dots.

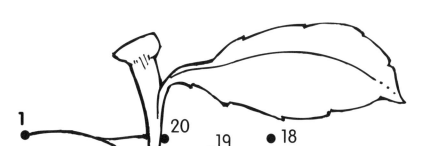

1

20
19
18
17

2

16

3

15

4

14

5

13

6

12

9
7
11
8
10

Center Activity

Note: Use this activity to review types of fruits and to introduce the term *orchard*.

Beanbag Toss

Creating the Center

1. Paint pictures of fruits on the posterboard. This is the "orchard."

2. Use the black marking pen to label each piece of fruit in the orchard.

3. Use your own beanbags or make simple ones by filling a child's sock with dry beans or popcorn kernels and sewing the ends together. Use the black marking pen to draw a farmer on the beanbags, as shown.

4. Place a strip of masking tape several feet away from the orchard.

Using the Center

1. Children stand several feet away from the orchard. Select one child to be the first player.

2. The child identifies the fruit he or she is aiming at and tosses the beanbag "farmer."

3. If the farmer lands on the item named, the child receives a counter. If it doesn't land on the item named, no counter is given.

4. Players take turns. The player with the most counters is the winner. (Or forget the counters and just play for fun!)

Extension

Make the center more challenging by requiring the players to choose cards containing pictures of the fruits on the playing mat and then to land on the item shown on the card.

Two children practice naming various types of fruit as they play this center game.

Materials

- large sheet of light brown posterboard

- permanent black marking pen

- tempera paint and paintbrushes

- beanbags

- masking tape

- counters (checkers, beans, etc.)

Note: Introduce the terms *hoe* and *crops* as you teach the song and movements. Sing this song to the tune of "The Mulberry Bush."

Outdoor and Music Activity

Teach the children to sing the following words as they pretend to be the farmer working on his farm. Then go to the playground and act out the song.

On My Farm

This is the way I plant the seeds,
Plant the seeds, plant the seeds.
This is the way I plant the seeds,
Early in the morning.

This is the way I water the plants,
Water the plants, water the plants.
This is the way I water the plants,
Early in the morning.

This is the way I hoe the weeds,
Hoe the weeds, hoe the weeds.
This is the way I hoe the weeds,
Early in the morning.

This is the way
    I pick the crops,
Pick the crops,
    pick the crops.
This is the way
    I pick the crops,
Early in the morning.

Alphabet Cards

Use these colorful Alphabet Cards in a variety of ways. Simply laminate and cut apart the cards and store them in a sturdy envelope or box.

Alphabet cards can be used to practice skills such as:

- letter recognition
- letter-sound association
- visual perception

Alphabet Card Games

What's My Name?   Use the alphabet cards to introduce the names of the letters, both uppercase and lowercase.

Make a Match   Children match a lowercase and uppercase letter. They then turn the cards over to self-check. If a correct match has been made, the child will see a picture of the same object whose name begins with the letter being matched.

First-Sound Game   Use the alphabet cards as phonics flash cards and ask children to identify the sound of each letter.

ABC Order   Children take all of the uppercase or lowercase cards and place them in alphabetical order.

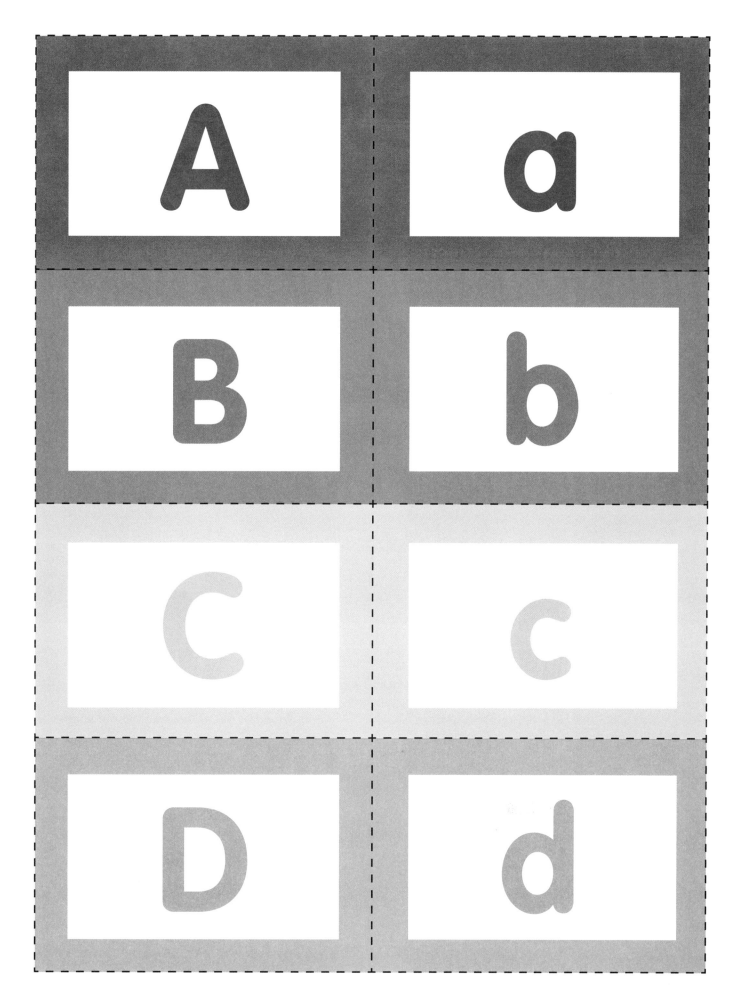

apple

Apple

barn

Barn

cow

Cow

duck

Duck

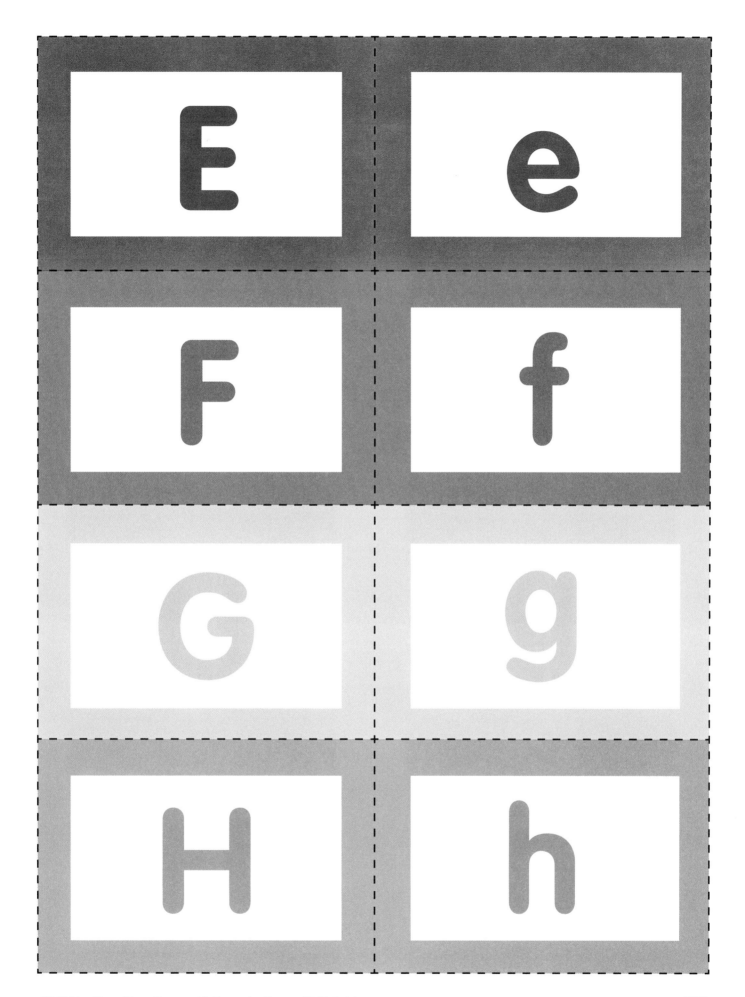

egg

Egg

farmer

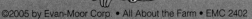

Farmer

gate

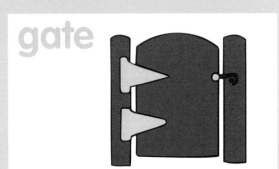

Gate

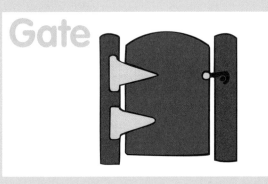

horse

Horse

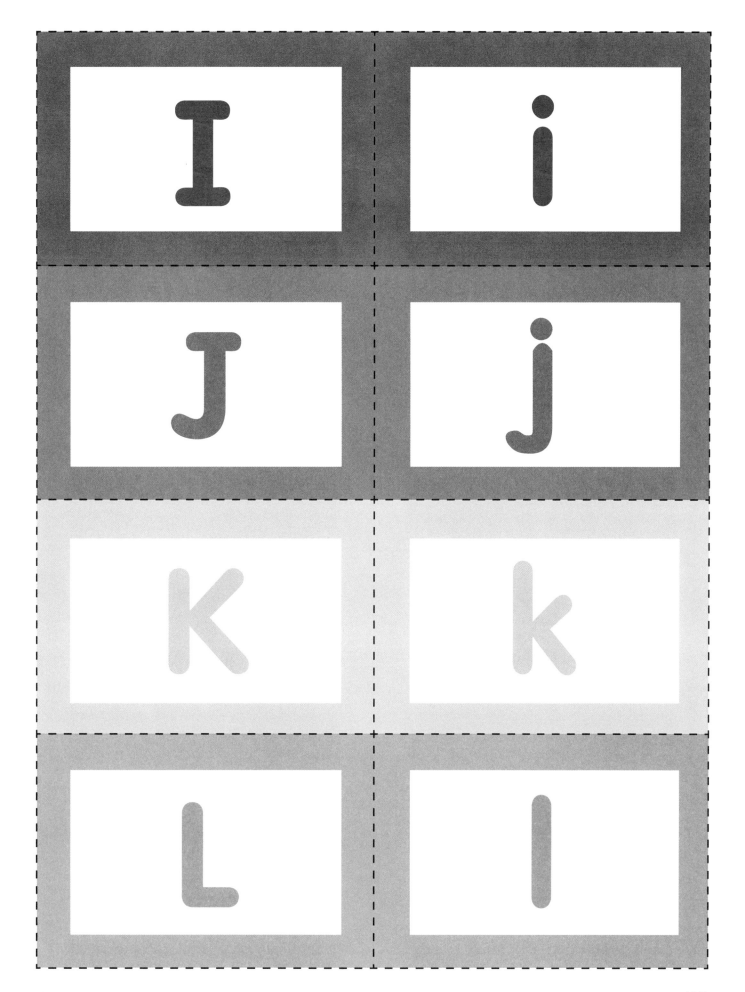

in the box

In the box

jam

Jam

kitten

Kitten

lamb

Lamb

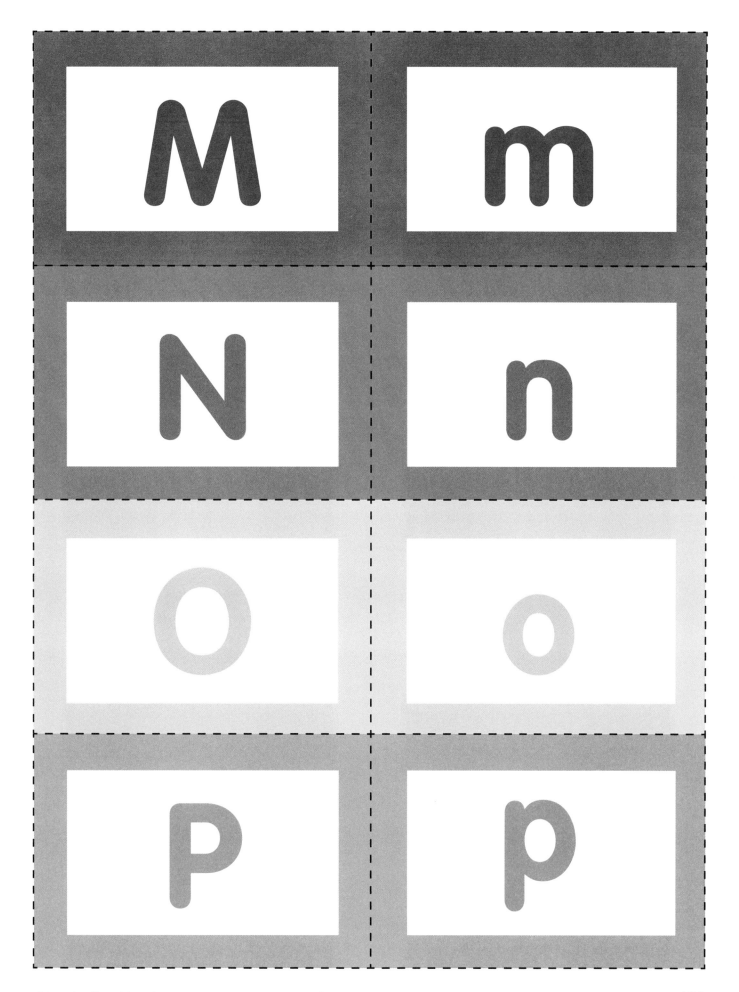

mouse

©2005 by Evan-Moor Corp. • All About the Farm • EMC 2402

Mouse

©2005 by Evan-Moor Corp. • All About the Farm • EMC 2402

nest

©2005 by Evan-Moor Corp. • All About the Farm • EMC 2402

Nest

©2005 by Evan-Moor Corp. • All About the Farm • EMC 2402

orange

©2005 by Evan-Moor Corp. • All About the Farm • EMC 2402

Orange

©2005 by Evan-Moor Corp. • All About the Farm • EMC 2402

pig

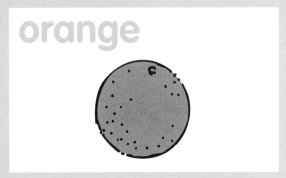

©2005 by Evan-Moor Corp. • All About the Farm • EMC 2402

Pig

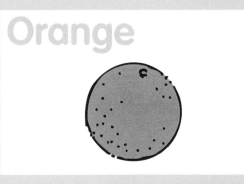

©2005 by Evan-Moor Corp. • All About the Farm • EMC 2402

Q q

R r

S s

T t

quilt

Quilt

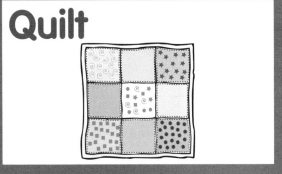

rooster

Rooster

seeds

Seeds

table

Table

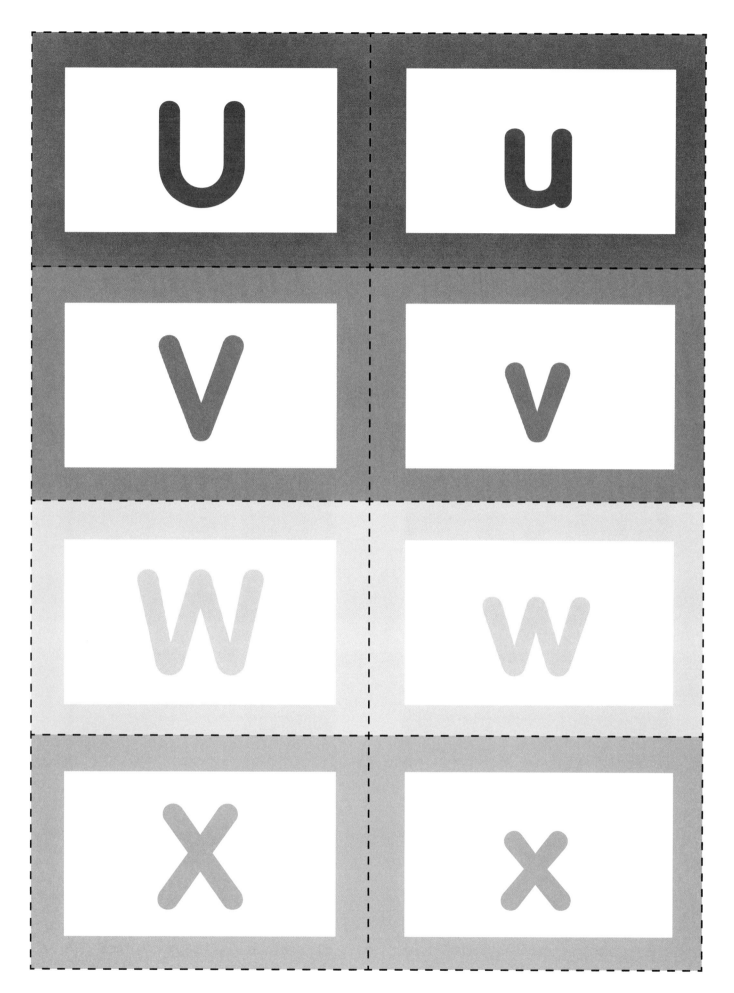

umbrella

Umbrella

vegetables

Vegetables

watermelon

Watermelon

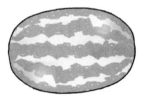

x on the barn door

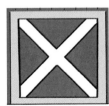

X on the barn door

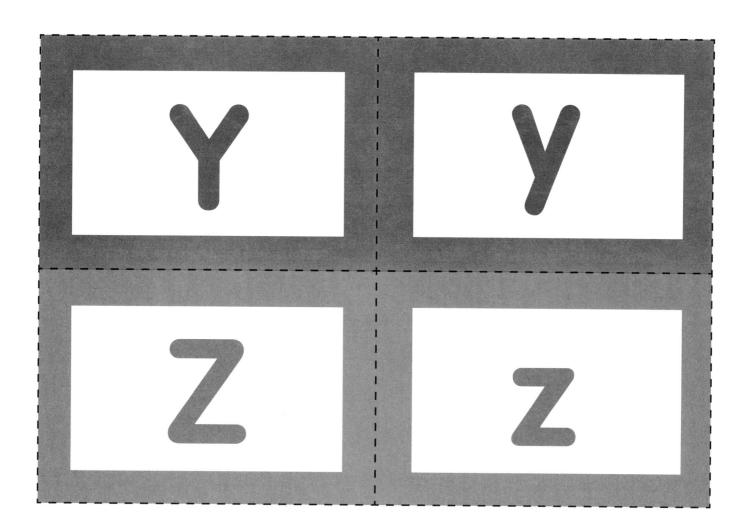

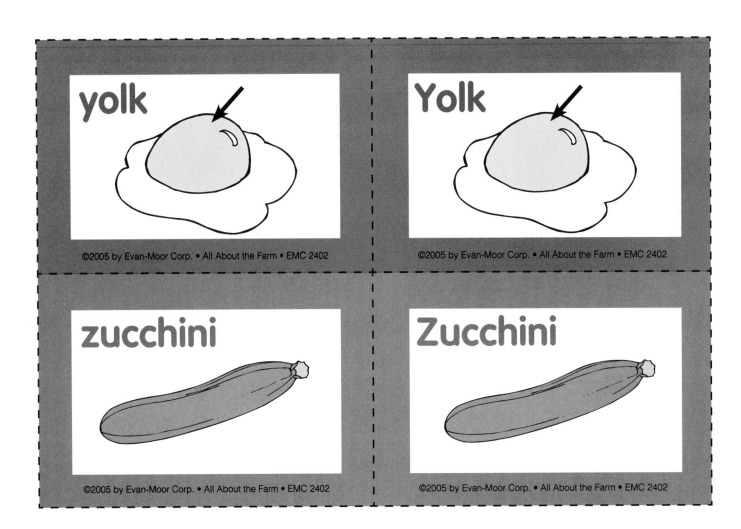

yolk

Yolk

zucchini

Zucchini

Answer Key

Page 28

Page 41

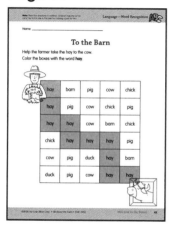

Page 42

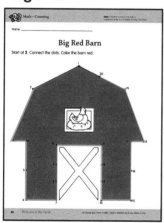

Page 43

There are 4 children.
There are 5 bales of hay.
There are 6 chicks.
There are 2 tractors.
There are 3 sheep.
There are 9 apples.

Page 68

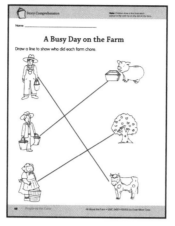

Page 79

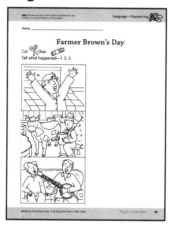

Page 80

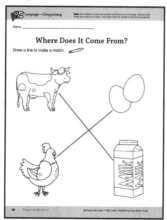

Page 81

Patterns will vary.

Page 82

Page 104

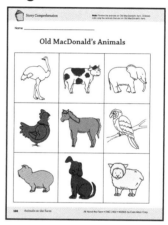

Page 115

Page 116

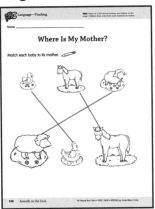

Page 117

Page 118

Page 144

Page 152

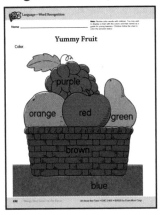

Page 153

Page 154

Page 155

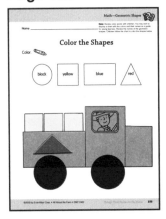

Page 159

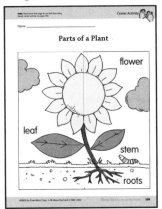

Page 178

Page 188

Page 189

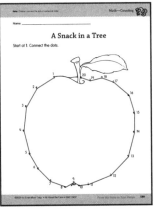